Somerset Legends

Somerset Legends

Berta Lawrence

David & Charles : Newton Abbot

GR
142
.S58L38
1973

Set in 11 on 13pt Plantin
and printed in Great Britain
by W J Holman Limited Dawlish
for David & Charles (Holdings) Limited
South Devon House Newton Abbot Devon

Contents

Illustrations

Introduction

The field of Somerset legend is a rich territory in which fact and fantasy are intermingled and not arranged in clearly defined strata. In many instances it is impossible to determine whether the legendary material originated in history or in imagination. Those who read the books and articles listed in the bibliography will find that, where authenticity of Somerset legends is concerned, the work of modern scholars and archaeologists can operate in two different ways: it can support or partly confirm stories and episodes embodied in legend—some of the Arthurian legends, for instance; or it can refute or demolish beliefs and theories upheld by traditional stories for centuries—an obvious example of which is the doubt cast on the legend of the Battle of Cynwit by the discovery of an early Christian burial-ground at Cannington Park, the legendary site of the battle. Local loyalties being strong, it takes a long time for evidence against the historical truth of a legend to be accepted, while confirmation is heartily welcomed. The writer, however, would not wish to suggest that the inhabitants of Somerset are so credulous today as to accept the more fanciful legends as literal truth or that she so accepts them herself.

These legends form part of a regional inheritance that inevitably is dwindling. A number have been vigorously maintained for centuries, more by oral tradition than by the written word, and most of these are still familiar knowledge and will remain so as long as certain landmarks and places endure; while others, as in many English counties, are drifting into oblivion and their recollection growing dimmer with successive generations. On the

7

other hand, certain Somerset legends exist mainly in the writings of long-dead scholars and in magazines and newspaper articles; the exploits of their central figures are sometimes illustrated by paintings or in stained-glass windows. The legends in this second class are less commonly known.

A book of this length does not permit investigation of sources and origins, nor any argument about varying or contradictory versions of a legend. On these two subjects the reader will find much useful information in the works listed in the bibliography.

Legends connected with fairy-lore have been omitted. There are many of these in Somerset, but they are vanishing from common memory more rapidly than the others. Legends of Exmoor, including those of the Doones, are also excluded. They would need a book of their own.

I

Saints

JOSEPH OF ARIMATHEA

The Hawthorn that groweth on Wirrall
Do burgen and bere grene leaves at Christmas
As fresh as other in May.

Ballad 1520

Wirrall Hill juts like a long steep peninsula into the flat lands south-west of Glastonbury that at one time lay under water. Perhaps its name means only 'peninsula' or 'promontory'. Or it may signify 'slope where bog-myrtle grows' or 'slope, meadow, where black horehound grows'. Whatever the meaning, Wirral or Worral is the hill's oldest name, although for nearly three centuries most people—including the makers of picture-postcards—have called it Wearyall Hill, because St Joseph of Arimathea and his companions were weary from their long pilgrimage when they rested on its summit.

This hill on the left of the Glastonbury–Bridgwater road (A39), as you leave Glastonbury behind, makes a high wind-swept field

9

where cattle graze. A few bushes tuft its slopes that are broken by curious humps suggestive of heaps of masonry overgrown with turf. On its ridge, but not on the highest point, a small ragged-looking tree leans sideways away from the winds that have so misshapen it. It is labelled 'A Glastonbury Holy Thorn' and looks as if cased in armour because a wire-and-metal cage protects it from cattle and vandals. At its foot a slab of grey lias, measuring 4ft 8in by 2ft 8in, lies embedded, so worn by weather that one can decipher only Ann Dom XXXII, the remains of an inscription erroneously informing the onlooker that Joseph of Arimathea reached Glastonbury in AD 32 instead of stating that he came '32 years after Christ's Passion', that is, about AD 63.

Mr John Clark of Bridgwater had this stone laid in the 1830s, near the place where the stump of an ancient thorn that still flowered valiantly had been grubbed up by the tenant of the land. Mr Clark himself loved the Holy Thorn legend without believing it. A later member of his family planted the present Holy Thorn at the time of King George V's Silver Jubilee. But the actual site of St Joseph's Thorn lies some distance further west, on the southern ridge of Wirrall about half a mile from Glastonbury; Hollar's map of 1676 indicates it by the words *Sacra Spina*, quite close to the road called Roman Road today, which overlies a real Roman road developed from a British track. Standing by the present Holy Thorn with your back to the traffic-laden A39, you look down on this road that for centuries was the main way leading out of Glastonbury towards Street, and see beyond it acres of low, lush pastures reclaimed from the old frequently-flooded marshes. Look left and you will get a memorable view of the abbey's lovely grey shell lying in the hollow of a valley backed by the Tor.

The stump whose site is marked by Mr Clark's stone was doubtless a scion of the Holy Thorn that had continued to stand on the edge of the Roman road until at least the end of the seventeenth century. Its gnarled torso had already split into two stout trunks when an Elizabethan Puritan sallied forth with axe and lantern to fell it on a dark night. His axe glanced off and gashed his leg; when he re-attacked the tree a chip of wood flew up and blinded him in one eye, so that he left the tree with one trunk incompletely severed as a small strip of bark still united it to the other. This trunk bloomed every Christmas for another thirty years while lying prone on the grass. When thrown into a ditch it budded defiantly until it was stolen. The second trunk vigorously threw out new boughs that spread like a round pavilion, putting forth green leaves and white blossoms every Christmas, because the potency of its sap prevailed against the constant breaking-off of twigs and branches, and the carving of names on its bark by hundreds of visitors. For many years it stood solitary on the otherwise treeless hill where cattle grazed in a great pasture. The frosts and severe cold of rigorous winters never harmed it. The cattle sheltered beneath the Thorn, trampling the ground bare and muddy all round it, going down on their knees in front of it, the story says, on Christmas Eve.

During the Civil War another Puritan cut this tree down, but long before this date scions of the tree flourished in many parts of Somerset—and elsewhere in England and even abroad, for there was a brisk trade in cuttings—in churchyards and gardens, from the Mendips to Whitestaunton and West Buckland. Two beautiful descendants stand in the grounds of Glastonbury Abbey and in the churchyard of St John the Baptist's church. The tree on the second Wirral site drew a crowd of pilgrims, in the middle of the eighteenth century, who testified that the holy tree remained indifferent to changes created by the new calendar, so that it broke into snowy bloom at midnight preceding *Old* Christmas Day (6 January) when the buds burst open with an audible crackle. Picking either buds or blooms brought bad luck. Today blossoms from Holy Thorns in Glastonbury deck the altar of the parish church at the season of Epiphany.

The legend of the original Holy Thorn remains as green and vigorous as did the tree beside the Roman road. It maintains that Joseph of Arimathea, who laid the body of Christ in his own tomb, voyaged with eleven missionary-disciples to convert the heathen British. Wearied by travel, they reached the top of Wirral Hill above the waters surrounding Ynyswitrin (Glastonbury) and were met by a hostile crowd of King Arviragus' subjects. Joseph, unmoved, struck his hawthorn staff into the ground where it took root, burgeoned and broke into blossom, thus proving the special blessedness of the foreign evangelists to the awestruck heathen and their ruler. From that day a sacred and venerated tree stood isolated on Wirral until the dawn of a new scepticism.

In Chester a brilliantly-painted sign for the Blossoms Inn portrays the red-cloaked saint on the green hill in front of his miraculously-flowering staff. It is curious that there is no similar sign in Somerset.

Which way did Joseph come? There are various legendary routes. The most reasonable one for him and his companions to follow was the sea-route along the coasts of Cornwall and Devon, up to the Severn Sea or Bristol Channel and thence to Glastonbury, sailing at the last stage of their voyage over great expanses of water, that shallowly covered nearly twenty miles of the present marsh-pastures and gave their later island-names to little elevated places like Godney and Beckery and a watery name to Meare. The heads of such islets, shaggy with rushes and willows, just overtopped the shallow sea that lapped the base of Wirral Hill where the immigrants could tie up their boat at the western end, where archaeologists have found traces of Roman wharves. They had received divine guidance to sail on until they saw across the waters a hill shaped like Tabor's holy mount; therefore Glastonbury Tor set their final course.

Yet many contend that Joseph's boat sailed out of the Severn Sea into the old estuary-harbour of Combwich and that the twelve missionaries used the ancient Parrett ford (still usable up to the beginning of the present century) to cross to the place now called Pawlett and then climbed up on to the ridgeway running along the Polden Hills. Or alternatively they reached this ridge-

way by using the long-forgotten loop of the river Parrett that ran
to a point under the small fortified camp at Downend, set on the
northern extremity of the ridge near Puriton village. They tied
up at a landing-stage that, like the river-loop, has been obliterated
by the making of the railway and various other developments,
although in its vicinity lies the modern Dunball wharf with its
cranes, seen on the A39 a mile or so north-east of Bridgwater.

Either way, Joseph's company tramped the ridgeway running
its straight course 300ft above the glistening meres and watery
marshes, past the places where today Loxley Woods and various
belts of trees make a green shade alongside the A39, on towards
Street and Glastonbury, beating a path that hundreds of pious
pilgrims to the shrines of Joseph and other saints would tread
during succeeding centuries, so that this track came to be called
the Pilgrims' Way. Just beyond the site of the present town of
Street, and not far from the modern sheepskin-factory sites of
Northover, the missionaries crossed the river Brue, not then
embanked, by an oaken bridge that was a forerunner of the
medieval *Pons Perilis* that came to be called Pomparles, the name
of the modern bridge. At low water they could use the new causeway of blue lias stone and oak timber that the Romans had constructed over the old British 'corduroy road' of peat overlaid with
boughs—as archaeological excavation revealed in 1880. This
causeway from Street to Glastonbury lay east of the present A39
and is now hidden by the turf. Afterwards the band of missionaries climbed up to the crest of Wirral Hill by the Roman road
mentioned earlier, part of the *Strata Via* that gave the town of
Street its name. The immigrants might well be weary.

The track, layered one-inch thick with small stones, ran north
of the present Polden road, behind the parkland of Knowle Hall
and the Knowle Inn. Although most of it is now lost under teasels
and brambles or covered by grassland, it is possible to walk part
of the Pilgrims' Way almost from its old starting-point. The
modern pilgrim will find the point nearest to it by travelling a
mile or so along the Bridgwater–Glastonbury road (A39) and at

Crandon Bridge, opposite the gates of Knowle Hall, taking the road marked 'Puriton'. This has recently been widened as an approach road to the M5 and climbs the slope of Puriton Hill between pastures on one side and woodland on the other. At the top, on the left, is an opening into a lane where for a short distance bungalows stand alongside a macadamised road shaded by fine trees. A space between trees reveals the wide misted plain spread below and cut by the great dyke called the King's Sedgemoor Drain carrying the waters of the river Cary towards the Parrett.

Soon the road becomes a rough broad way overhung by beeches and sycamores swagged with ivy that make an untrimmed woodland belt from a place on the left where a gate marked NO ENTRY opens on a path descending to several burning lime-kilns. The way opens out on an uneven grassy clearing that provides an outlook towards Puriton church tower, village roofs and a tower of the Royal Ordnance Factory. Untidy wild flowers and weeds riot along the verge and, appropriately in a place walked by Joseph, a number of hawthorns stand between the taller trees. The track ends abruptly in a spur jutting over a grey Gehenna of motorway roadworks (in 1972), a scooped-out hollow floored with dark debris. At one time the Pilgrims' Way ran further out over land that has vanished, nearer to the river Parrett, seen broadening out and winding its turgid waters towards Bridgwater and Combwich. From the tip of the Pilgrims' Way you can see near Combwich a dark patch marking Cannington Park, and behind it the mistier, loftier outline of Danesborough—both historic camps. You must imagine the river-loop that brought Joseph to a landing-place somewhere below this viewpoint.

Across the approach-road outside the lane's entry another section of the Pilgrims' Way is visible, running between woodlands behind Knowle Hall to pursue a more sheltered course than the nearly parallel A39.

There is another traditional route of Joseph's, less commonly known but firmly held in local opinion as the true one. Even the unimaginative sense something 'lost' and mysterious when they follow it, for it lies well away from frequented roads and is identified by ancient natural landmarks. Its focal point is Wick Hollow, or the little hamlet of Wick at the foot of Stonedown Hill on which, perhaps, there stood some prehistoric sacred stones. You may approach the place by Well House Lane, near Chalice Well, in the higher part of Glastonbury, climbing Stonedown Hill, where beautiful ashes and beeches shade Stonedown Fields and the top affords a sight of the Tor with its falling terraced sides, and then walking downhill to follow the lefthand lane at its foot. Alternatively, climb up to Bove Town, 'above' Glastonbury, pass through an area marked Wick Hollow, where new houses mingle with old cottages on the steep banks, and make your way to Norwood Park Farm, passing stone barns and Avalonian apple orchards and the ephemeral homes of today's hippie-pilgrims. From the farm, a lane roughly paved with grass-overgrown stones and overhung by ash, sycamore, elderberry and hawthorn, that splash vivid colours in autumn, leads on to rougher and stonier Stonedown Drove. If Joseph and his followers walked over Stonedown and down the fossil-strewn drove, they made for the ancient lane on the right at the bottom of Stonedown—when you approach from Norwood Park Farm—that today is darkened by drooping and intertwined branches, and so entangled with briars, bushes and rank hedgerow-plants as to be almost impenetrable. The persistent explorer fights his way to an emptier, sunken stretch of lane, bordered by a deep ditch, darkly shaded, narrow, muddy—it is part of an ancient track—close to the orchard of Wick Farm; from where it can, of course, be more easily approached, although this involves trespassing on private land.

The Mecca of this pilgrimage today are the two Oaks of Avalon, vast and scaly monsters called Gog and Magog who guard the orchard entrance and, in spite of their renewed foliage, look as if the burden of their estimated 2,000 years is breaking them down to final decay. Joseph of Arimathea saw them in their pride of youth as part of a great oak grove at Stonedown's foot, sacred to druidical or some other pagan worship. He saw too a fine avenue of oaks that led him towards the Tor, before he made his way to Wirral via a track that is now Paradise Lane, north of the Tor. Yet it is just as likely that, instead of walking over Stonedown, Joseph's missionaries rowed over the waters to Wick, for it is situated at sea-level and the sea lapped just below the oaks' standing-place.

Fifteen paces are needed for walking round either Gog or Magog. It is a strange little experience to stand on those writhen roots and lay a hand on that knotted, half-rotted body with its 40ft circumference and scores of annular rings. Almost the entire grove and avenue were felled in 1906. By 1935 only Gog, Magog and a fellow-giant still stood. This third oak was felled in 1937 and a Glastonbury craftsman used its wood, of a warm red colour, to make bowls, candlesticks and a 'Glastonbury chair' of the traditional pattern.

King Arviragus made the foreign missionaries a substantial grant of land, known for centuries as the Twelve Hides of Glastonbury. They settled as holy hermits in a colony of tiny wattle-and-daub cells at the base of the Tor, not far from the well, now called Chalice Well, which supplied their water. But first they built the earliest Christian church in Britain, the little oratory where the light of the gospel burned all through the darkest ages, maintaining a small flame even when the isle called Ynyswitrin became no more than a shelter for wild beasts after Joseph's death. They constructed it with mud and wreathed alder twigs—'wands winded and intertwined'—from the adjoining marshes that also provided rushes to thatch its roof. It measured 60ft by 26ft and had three windows on each side, one at the west end and one at the east over the altar. One of its two doors reached the low eaves. Joseph of Arimathea himself carved for it a wooden image of the Blessed Virgin to whom it was dedicated. This was 'the church of boughs', the *vetusta ecclesia* or 'old church' that became one of the most renowned shrines in Christendom. Early in the seventh century St Paulinus, a Saxon bishop, had this frail wicker casket encased in timber and lead. In 1184 it perished in the fire that consumed almost the entire abbey; Joseph's image of the Virgin survived.

The Life of Joseph of Arimathea, printed in 1520, tells us:

> So Joseph dyd as the aungell him bad
> And wrought there an ymage of our lady
> . . . .
> And that same ymage is yet at Glastonbury

The monks mourned the loss of the wattle oratory more than that of the great abbey church and built on its exact site an exquisite Lady Chapel of the same dimensions. They brought cream-coloured stone from Doulting for building and local blue lias stone for the capitals and decorative details, which were superbly ornamented with sculptured patterns, geometric, floral, foliate. A later abbot excavated a crypt beneath the floor in order to make an underground Chapel of St Joseph, where he set a stone image of Joseph of Arimathea at the east end on a pedestal near the north wall. Fresh legends grew around this building. A Norman arch decorated with elaborate billet-ornament was constructed round an ancient well in the crypt that was eagerly sought out by pilgrims since it was St Joseph's Well—the name it bears today —whose healing water cured eye ailments and many other ills. Today it is reached from the Lady Chapel by a flight of steps deeply hollowed by pilgrims' feet. A grille covers the well, but there is now only a small gleam of water.

Even as a roofless ruin the Lady Chapel presents a miracle of architectural beauty, with its Romanesque north door and west window, both elaborately sculptured. The entire building is generally referred to as St Joseph's Chapel.

The night after his arrival at Glastonbury Joseph is said to have had a vision in which the archangel Gabriel commanded him to build a church in honour of the Mother of God. In a second vision Joseph saw Christ himself descend to consecrate

17

St Joseph's Well, Glastonbury; a vignette from Phelps's *Antiquities of Somersetshire*

the church to the Virgin; this legend, and another, supports the statement that no human hands ever dedicated the *vetusta ecclesia*.

On the eastern side of Mendip in a green bower of trees lies Pilton, approached by the A361 from Glastonbury. Its territory covers several square miles of irregular up-and-down landscape composed of hillsides dipping into unexpected hollows and valleys before finally levelling out. Main roads and houses inside walled gardens occupy high ground above the church that is sheltered in a valley yet considerably elevated above the land lying south of it, where the manor house was built on the site of a summer dwelling for Abbots of Glastonbury. The burnt-out walls of the fine monastic tithe barn stand on another higher level

18

opposite the church's south door. The lowest land is traversed by a glinting willow-edged stream, which at a place called Steanbow, between Pilton and West Pennard, was spanned by a medieval bridge, and doubtless earlier bridges. Springs create numerous brooks that run across this low-lying territory to fill such Sedgemoor rivulets as Redlake and Whitelake. There is a little ford, and waterfalls, not far from the church. Here again are moorland acres that Joseph of Arimathea saw inundated by the sea. In the dip under the main village and the church, reached by a road dropping down to cross a grey stone bridge overhung by ash and willow, the sea branched inward to make a tidal creek, or 'pill', which was used as a harbour and gave Pilton its name.

When the inhabitants of Pilton learned that missionaries had brought a new religion to Ynyswitrin and that King Arviragus himself had embraced it, they begged Joseph to extend his preaching beyond the boundary of the Twelve Hides of Glastonbury so that they might be similarly blessed.

The missionaries therefore carried the gospel to Pilton, where Joseph built a second mud-and-wattle church in a sheltered hollow above the reach of the waters, and baptised his converts by immersion in a creek. The site of this wattle church is covered by the little Lady chapel in the north aisle of the present church at Pilton. The former boundary line of Glastonbury Twelve Hides runs through this church, in at the Norman south door and out at the north. In a decorated recess, with ball-flower ornament on the moulding of one of its arches, an Easter sepulchre of unusual design can be seen. Instead of having an effigy recumbent on it, the flat slab of the stone tomb chest is ornamented by the head of Christ encased within the head of a foliated cross.

Many believe that Joseph, the Christian missionary, came to a country in some degree familiar to him, because during the previous forty years he had made two or three expeditions with other metal-merchants to Cornwall for tin and to Somerset for

lead. He made the first of his trade-voyages to the Mendip region
when quite a young man, bringing with him his great-nephew,
Jesus of Nazareth, a carpenter's son in his early teens who helped
him as shipwright. They tied up their boat at the landing-stage
by Pilton creek and bought lead from the miners who came down
from Priddy and Charterhouse-on-Mendip. This story is depicted on the banner hanging in the Lady Chapel at Pilton.
Jesus, haloed with gold, in a red garment, stands in the boat with
Joseph and another merchant. Glastonbury Tor rises in the background but unfortunately the embroiderers set the Tower of St
Michael's church, built in the Middle Ages, on top of the Tor
for easier identification.

It is said that Joseph of Arimathea, or one of his disciples, built
a reed-thatched oratory—and later Christians their Lady chapel
—on the place where the Christ Child knelt to pray after dis-
embarking.

Others think that the boy Jesus made several journeys to
Somerset with Joseph and that on two occasions they came, as an
old Chapbook relates, to the place now called Burrowbridge.
They would have sailed out of Bridgwater Bay into harbour at
Combwich, pronounced 'Cummidge'—reached nowadays by the
Hinkley Point road off the A39 at Cannington, three miles west
of Bridgwater—and then up the soil-brown tidal river Parrett to
Burrow bridge, where at that time the tributary river Cary,
rising near Castle Cary, flowed into it. The Cary now enters the
Parrett at Dunball, below Bridgwater, having been cut and
straightened—or, one might say, short-circuited at Henley
Corner—in 1791, to make the great dyke called the King's
Sedgemoor Drain. This important engineering feat helped to
drain the wide marshes, whose watery character is made apparent
by frequent streaks of flood water on the lush pastures, by
patches of soggy black peat and by the silvery glint of water in
the straight willow-fringed rhines, or ditches, cut for drainage.

Joseph and the boy Jesus, following their course up the river
Cary, would have landed near the little place now called Beer, a

hamlet in the parish of High Ham, on the Bridgwater–Langport road A372. From there they walked to Glastonbury, along a beautiful route that can still be followed. From a corner where Beer is marked on a signpost, the road starts to climb steeply past farms whose thatch is green with moss, past hayricks and barns, between banks overhung by trees, continually turning and twisting in sharp hairpin bends to the summit of Turn Hill—locally called Ham Hill and not to be confused with Ham or Hamdon Hill, famous for its quarries of golden stone, not far from Yeovil. Partly clothed by the lovely Ham woods stretching as far as Aller, Turn Hill stands 300ft above the moor, commanding a tremendous prospect of Sedgemoor and the Vale of Taunton, backed by the misted range of the Quantocks, with the Poldens lying northward. Several acres of the hill are National Trust property, where picnic parties come in summer; but even as early as February it is a pleasure to walk here, to tread the carpets of crisp bronzed beech leaves, to come upon thorn-bushes garlanded with black ivy-berries and their glossy foliage, and to find yellow-dusted catkins pendent on alder and hazel.

Joseph with the boy Jesus climbed some tortuous trackway, the forerunner of the present road, passed through dense woods and onward to the site of High Ham village, then descended to Henley and, by some slightly raised marshland track or irregularly-placed stepping stones, to the site of the present larger hamlet Pedwell. Still today the road and its small bridges over King's Sedgemoor Drain stand somewhat raised above the reedy flat lands. Then the route goes on to the Polden ridgeway at Ashcott (A39) and to Glastonbury.

Forty years ago a shepherd in those steep fields on Turn Hill slopes could point out a green path which, he told walkers, was used by Joseph of Arimathea. The place where two of these paths intersected is, according to legend, the site of the present beautiful High Ham church near the village green.

But the most deeply-rooted of all the legends about journeys of the boy Jesus to Somerset, and one that has passed into the national canon, is his visit to Priddy, that cold, windswept village on the high open top of Mendip that looks to far horizons. In those pre-Roman times, the heights of Mendip carried acres of dense forest, and the mining-industry was small and primitive, the mines being shallow trenches. To imagine the scene, one must forget the shafts, the ruined chimneys, the grass-grown heaps of waste, the areas of 'gruffy' ground—visible evidence of the lead-mining industry that developed, flourished and died. Nevertheless, walking that exposed and lonely plateau one sees much that Jesus might have seen in AD 15: endless grey stone walls; clumps of ash trees; lonely pools; fields strewn and ribbed with limestone, and pocked in places by swallet-holes whence issues the strange voice of subterranean streams finding their way through a honeycomb of caverns. The boy Jesus looked also on those impressive centuries-old landscape features that today bring many visitors to Priddy: the four inexplicable earthen circles, each with a diameter of 550ft, in a field near the Castle of Comfort Inn, and the two groups of Bronze Age barrows, reached by following Nine Barrows Lane out of the village. These are the group of nine huge bowl-barrows, called Priddy Nine Barrows, and their neighbours on Ashen Hill, where eight great bowl-barrows swell above the turf of a field walled and scattered with stones. Here He could have stood under the spacious sky and the soaring larks, whose song even today is often the only sound to break the silence.

'As sure as our Lord came to Priddy' was an expression used in North Somerset until the present century. The modern traveller comes from Glastonbury to Priddy via Wells and Old Bristol Road which climbs steeply between tall hedges, spinneys and ivy-grown banks starred in spring by primroses.

A strongly-rooted legend asserts that Jesus spent several of his unchronicled youthful years in Glastonbury, talking with scholars and priests of Druidical faith—a religion of which little is known —who lived in a small community on the Tor. Sometimes he moved among common people like the wild Priddy miners and the Glastonbury fishermen and fowlers. He knew the remarkable, artistically gifted inhabitants of the two Lake Villages, people who wove, fished, farmed, built boats and carts, made basketwork and ironwork as well as pottery, jewellery and mirrors of great beauty and skilled design. They were to perish about thirty years later. And above all, during this sojourn, Jesus himself built the little church of mud-and-wattle and consecrated it to his Mother.

The lingering of this story in people's minds is illustrated by several lines from a contemporary verse-drama by Maurice Broadbent:

> The boy wandered with the Brythons. They took him
> To the Isle of Glass which is their most holy spot
> And there he built a house of boughs
> And twisted wickerwork, and passed his time
> With their young students.

A legend of St David depends on two of the legends about the wattle church. Founder of monasteries and Bishop of Menevia—which became St David's in Pembrokeshire—David came with several bishops to Glastonbury in AD 530, just after presiding at a Synod where onlookers saw a dove with a golden beak perched on his shoulder and whispering in his ear. Artists have portrayed St David with his dove. At Glastonbury David intended to repair monastic buildings that lay in partial decay, but first of all he would re-consecrate the old wattle church to the Virgin. During the night before the ceremony, Christ appeared to David in a dream and forbade re-consecration because he himself had dedicated the wattle church to his Mother and human hands must not repeat his action. Christ touched the palm of David's hand with his forefinger and as an immediate sign a small hole pierced the palm. Christ told David that during his celebration of the Mass, at the moment he recited 'per Ipsum et cum Ipso et in Ipso', the wound would vanish. We are told that preparation for a consecration came to nothing and the hole in David's palm, seen by an awed congregation, disappeared at the appointed time. Then David built a new wooden church, east of the wattle church, and dedicated it to the Blessed Virgin, setting up a pillar in the old churchyard to show future generations where Joseph of Arimathea's oratory had stood, 'lest the place of the former church should be forgotten'. The foundations of this pillar are believed to have been found during excavation in 1921.

When David travelled to Jerusalem, the Patriarch urged him to convert the heathen and presented him with a bell, a staff and a consecrated portable altar such as missionaries carried. David adorned this with a wonderful sapphire and presented it to his church at Glastonbury. Later abbots added other jewels to 'David's sapphire altar'. This was the altar 'garnished with silver and gilte, called the great sapphire of Glassenbury' that fell into the hands of Henry VIII. David was at Glastonbury when the wounded Arthur, who was a kinsman, was carried there for healing. It is said that four centuries after St David's death his bones were translated to Glastonbury to rest in the *vetusta ecclesia*.

Joseph of Arimathea made other trade-expeditions to Somerset after the Romans' arrival in AD 44 for they quickly improved the mining industry on Mendip. He came to the harbour at Uphill, now a suburb of Weston-super-Mare, and was rowed in a smaller boat up the River Axe. Rising in a hidden ferny place at Priddy, the river goes underground on Mendip and emerges through the rocks in the deepest recesses of Wookey Hole cavern to escape into daylight and flow down to meet the Severn Sea, where Uphill looks across to the headland of Brean Down. An exposed breezy hill rises 100ft above the site of the former old village of Uphill spread along the Axe's northern bank. Here the ruined church of St Nicholas looks out on the little river-mouth port the Romans named *Ad Axium* and on its sheltering headland. According to legend, the Norman builders, who had begun to erect a church down in the valley, found their work undone when they arrived in the early morning; during the night St Nicholas had carried their blocks of stone up to the hilltop as a sign that he wanted his church to provide a landmark for mariners.

Joseph of Arimathea waited on this muddied shore for the traders to bring down their laden pack-animals from Priddy and Charterhouse. Some maintain that he travelled down with them after trading on Mendip top, where the miners carried out their smelting on stone hearths and used clay crucibles to extract a little silver from their lead, although they wasted much valuable material, as their refuse-heaps have proved. In any case Joseph grew familiar with the new Roman road that replaced the track Jesus had used when he came that way. This Roman road has been traced some fifty miles from Old Sarum in Wiltshire to Uphill, and part of it is faintly visible where it passes through the mysterious Priddy circles near the Castle of Comfort, a section known as 'the potters' road' along which lead was fetched for glazing pottery.

Thus Somerset harbours and trackways, the harsh winds and rains of Mendip, the swirling mists of the marshes round Ynyswitrin, the boggy causeways, the waterways of the Parrett, Brue, Axe and Cary were already known to Joseph when he came as missionary with eleven companions.

Joseph of Arimathea died somewhere in Ynyswitrin at a patriarchal age on 27 July AD 82, and the Glastonbury monks always kept his feast on that day. He was buried with great honour, either in his own wattle chapel near the well in its Norman recess under the south wall or, as many believe, outside its south corner in the churchyard that, because it was Joseph's resting-place, became filled to a depth of 16ft with the bones of saints, monks and kings, and came to be called 'the holiest earth in England', in which it was a privilege to lie.

One curiously dissentient legend, entirely lacking in detail, states that Joseph of Arimathea has his grave on the great forti- fied settlement called Hamdon Hill, or Ham Hill, near Stokesub-Hamdon. For centuries, the lovely yellow Ham stone was quarried from its flanks to build churches, stately homes like Montacute House and Barrington Court, and farmhouses over a wide area of Somerset, as well as entire villages, very beautiful, in the Yeovil district. How could Joseph's grave have been identified? The remains of both Briton and Roman have been found there, including a British warrior's skeleton. The Roman Fosse Way passes through the north end of the village.

This legendary site of Joseph's grave seems to link with a little-known story that he founded a tiny Christian settlement at Crewkerne and died when visiting it from Glastonbury. On his arrival as evangelist to Britain, it is said that he sailed with his eleven companions into harbour late one night on the Dorset coast, and as they were weary they slept in the boat. Peasants emerged from their clay huts and, looking down from the cliffs, saw the full moon shining on something near Joseph's hand that threw back a silvery beam. Next day the twelve came ashore, each carrying a wooden cross, and followed a traders' path along the western bank of the river Brit, which at that time flowed in a more easterly direction. The peasants crowded round in hostility, brandishing rude spears and shouting threats. Joseph held up either the metal cup, that was later called the Grail, or perhaps a silver vial containing drops of Christ's blood, that is, a 'cruet' like the pair so often portrayed in association with Joseph. At once the people became friendly, brought offerings of cheese, honey and bread, and gave the missionaries shelter. The missionaries preached the gospel, and when they moved on one of them left his rood, or wooden cross, standing in the ground to be revered as the symbol of the new faith. Beneath the earthwork of Conegar, near the modern Bridport, they repeated these actions then journeyed on, quelling enmity by holding up the cup, preaching and leaving their roods standing at eleven places until, utterly weary, they reached Wirral Hill above the flooded winter island of Ynyswitrin, where Joseph planted his own wooden cross and it flowered. Their route from Crewkerne in Somerset, close to the present

Dorset border, took them through places that are now Martock, Long Load, Long Sutton, Somerton and so to Street by a Roman road.

On his tomb, his disciples set this inscription:

> Ad Britannos veni
> post Christum sepelvi.
> Docui. Quievi.

('I came to the Britons after I buried Christ. I taught. I am at rest.')

Buried with him at Glastonbury were two precious slenderly-shaped silver vessels or 'cruets', containing blood and sweat from Christ's Passion, that Joseph had brought from Palestine and placed on the altar of his wattle church. The image of these two cruets became, like the flowering thorn, a symbol of the saint and in church iconography a much more frequent one. Its later representation in stained glass, in sculptured stone and carved wood, was largely due to the great abbot-builder Richard Beere, who adopted the two cruets on a shield as his own heraldic device, thus showing his special devotion to St Joseph of Arimathea. He set this, with the initials RB, on a number of churches and abbey-barns that he built; sometimes people have mistakenly and impolitely referred to the cruets as Abbot Beere's beer-jugs. They are also carved on a corbel shield on the south side of the nave in St Benedict's church at Glastonbury; on a gable end of the beautiful and interesting little chapel of St Patrick belonging to the women's almshouses—recently demolished—inside the gates of Glastonbury Abbey; on the south side of the chancel arch at Meare; on the great abbey barns at Glastonbury and Doulting; and on a wall of the manor house at Sharpham. They are also carved on oak bench-ends in North Cadbury church.

In the noble parish church of St John the Baptist at Glastonbury they are portrayed in the sixteenth-century stained glass of the south window, where they appear in the lower quarters of a shield that is splashed with red blood-drops. Between the cruets stands a green cross, sharply notched like the branches of a raggedly-trimmed thorn-tree. And in Langport church, not far from Ham Hill and Beer that hold such strong associations with him, Joseph appears in the medieval glass of the twelve-light window crowded with saints. He wears rich Eastern dress and carries the two cruets on a white cloth on his palm. The figure of Joseph, with the cruets, is also painted on the panel of the screen in the church at Plymtree in Devon.

For centuries Joseph's bones lay either under the floor of the wattle church or, as is more commonly believed, outside and south of it in the monks' cemetery, filled with illustrious dead. Over the years its identity was obliterated, but early in the fourteenth century a man, who claimed to have received a revelation in a dream, obtained the king's permission to dig for Joseph's remains inside the abbey precincts and 'the bodies of Joseph of Arimathea and his companions were found at Glastonbury'. The sacred bones of Joseph were enclosed most reverently in a silver casket and placed in a richly-decorated shrine, the base of which was a sarcophagus of stone with sculptured ornament. From this stone base the casket could be raised for the adoration of the countless pilgrims who made 'the journey to Joseph of Arimathee'. Joseph's shrine stood in the middle of the sanctuary at the east end of the crypt called St Joseph's Chapel in which his stone statue presided, and it drew the faithful from far beyond Somerset to pray, make their offerings, and to benefit from miracles of healing and assistance. These blessings were bestowed on people of every rank, from Robert Brown, a poor escaped prisoner from Yeovil whose iron fetter fell off, to Mrs Lyte, the lady of Lytes Cary—now a National Trust property—who was cured of quartan fever. Two afflicted girls from Doulting, who came to pray at the shrine on the day of SS Simon and Jude, were both healed. Crippled Alice Bennett of Wells limped into St Joseph's Chapel and, after prayers before the shrine, found that she could leave her crutches there and walk out. It became one of the most renowned shrines in Christendom.

Some of the pilgrims who died while at Glastonbury were

buried in the much-coveted place under the Chapel floor, where excavation revealed their coffined skeletons with their pilgrim staffs of holly and hazel lying alongside them.

At the time of the Reformation the gold-and-silver-decked shrine was plundered and broken up by desecrating hands. Only the flat altar-tomb, that had held the moveable silver casket, remained in St Joseph's ruined chapel, gazed on by curious visitors. There it stayed for over 120 years until, one dark night, a number of pious people, and it needed a number, moved it so hastily yet with such difficulty that the stonework suffered damage. They placed it in the churchyard of the church of St John the Baptist, outside the east end of St Mary's Chapel, where it remained for over 200 years, deeply sunk into the turf and greened over with moss. It has stood now for nearly fifty years in St Catherine's Chapel within the church of St John the Baptist. This splendid altar-tomb is very richly sculptured with bands of ornament. Each of the sculptured panels—four on each side, one at each end—encloses a quatrefoil. One can decipher the initials JA, which sceptics say stand for a John Alleyne of Glastonbury, although they have not proved it. A worn and straggling design, almost obliterated by the ravages of weather out in the churchyard, is seen by some as a twig of ragged thorn, by others as the snake-twined caduceus of Mercury. The monument is one of the most treasured possessions among a number of beautiful objects in this church. Of the many people who come here, few fail to touch the sculptured stonework, thinking that the remains of the plinth inside may have supported the receptacle enclosing St Joseph's hallowed bones.

The cruets were never found. Some say they will be, others that the plunderers took them. There is one odd little story that in extreme old age Joseph gave them into the keeping of his great-nephew Isaac, who had joined him at Ynyswitrin. Many years later, when Isaac felt his life endangered by the hostility of some of the pagan Roman conquerors, he hid the two cruets inside an old hollow fig tree, which he cast into the sea off the

Somerset coast, trusting God to bring them to a safe place. The sea carried them over to Gaul, to the place called Fécamp where eventually an abbey was built that cherished these holy relics.

And the Grail? The story that Joseph of Arimathea brought with him to Britain the cup used at the Last Supper, which contained drops of the Saviour's blood, is a much later legend and in many particulars not one that belongs specially to Somerset. It maintains, however, that Joseph was bearing the sacred cup when he reached Wearyall Hill and that he concealed it in some stony nook under the waters of Chalice Well, which became so reddened by the blood that the well assumed a second name, the Blood Spring. Down the years, hundreds of people have believed the miraculous event of this well-loved legend. Many do not reject it even today, though philologists point out that Chilkwell Street, which runs past the well, was formerly Chalcewell Street. The name 'Chalice Well' is therefore a false formation of the original, which accurately denoted a chalybeate spring, that is, a spring containing iron. This iron reddens the water which, in turn, leaves red stains like congealed blood on the surfaces it runs over.

In the eighteenth century new stories originated about the Blood Spring's wonderful healing powers; scores of people from North Wootten, West Pennard, Chew Magna and many other Somerset places gave sworn testimony that drinking its water had cured their serious illnesses. This led to the building of a small spa at Glastonbury and to a short-lived period when thousands sought the Blood Spring's miraculous help. The Spa House, transformed to a private dwelling, stands in Magdalene Street on the opposite side to the abbey grounds.

Chalice Well has been devotedly cared for and attracts thousands of visitors. Even those who doubt the legend of the chalice know that, as this is Glastonbury's most powerful spring, the colony of little clay-and-wattle cells raised by Joseph and his fellows must have clustered near it, in the shadow of the Tor. The well is now inside the terraced garden behind Chalice Well

House, and is approached via Well House Lane at the foot of the Tor. The spring over which it is built rises in a deep depression between the Tor and Chalice Hill, with its girdle of apple-orchards, and sends a stream flowing along a paved course for some distance down Chilkwell Street, then down Bere Lane towards the abbey barn. The spring supplied the abbey's water. It yields 1,000 gallons every hour and in the driest summer never fails.

After descending the three steps to lean over the curiously marked stonework of Chalice Well's circular rim, the visitor hears the furious groaning noise of this ever-gushing spring within its stone chamber down below the stone cover. He drinks his cup of water and finds it ice-cold and iron-flavoured on his tongue. All around the stonework the water makes an accumulation of rusty-red stains and encourages the growth of masses of red-brown fungi.

Or was the cup that Joseph, and later the abbey, so reverently cherished a small bowl of olive wood, about five inches in diameter, with tapering base? Such a cup, its wood darkened by the years, its rim roughened by those who drank from it in search of healing, was preserved for many years by the Powell family at Nanteos. Many believe that seven Glastonbury monks carried it there after vainly trying to lodge it safely in the Cistercian abbey at Strata Florida when Henry VIII demanded Glastonbury's treasures.

The Grail figures as a gold chalice, with two gold cruets, in the top lights of a window in St Catherine's Chapel of the church of St John the Baptist, Glastonbury. The modern stained glass (1936) of this window portrays various scenes from the life of Joseph of Arimathea. Here the saint stands robed in violet, carrying the two cruets. Here he is seen with the blue-robed Virgin at the embalmment of Christ's body. Here he is painted bringing the cruets to Glastonbury, with an excited crowd coming to meet him, and a ship with a single lug sail in the background. And here he is portrayed planting his hawthorn staff on

Wearyall Hill while King Arviragus, son of Cymbeline, watches.

Near the altar in the chancel there are two windows filled with fifteenth-century glass, and in one of these there is a much earlier painted symbol recalling Joseph's legendary life in Somerset; a small green cross of hawthorn in company with Tudor roses.

A century earlier some delicate-fingered artist carved the Virgin holding a blossoming hawthorn on an ivory seal for Glastonbury Abbey.

ALDHELM

Aldhelm, whom Llewelyn Powys called the most lovable of Saxon saints, possessed every quality of the great churchman and the illustrious scholar, combined with humanity and tenderness towards men of every rank. By his faith and eloquence he led many souls out of pagan darkness and he exerted over his kinsman Ina, King of Wessex, an influence powerful enough to persuade him to rebuild the church at Glastonbury, demolished by the Saxon invaders, and, tradition holds, to build the first church at Wells, of timber or even of cob-and-thatch, on a site south of the present cathedral. King Ina created Aldhelm successively Abbot of Malmesbury and the first Bishop of Sherborne. Members of Aldhelm's wealthy family owned practically all the lands of east Somerset, while his see included the whole of Dorset and Somerset, and extended into Wiltshire. These few historical 'bones' support the body of Aldhelm legends. The Somerset legends belong mainly to the eastern half of the county.

Aldhelm's diocese of Sherborne was described as being situated 'west of Selwood', a reference to the dense forest of Selwood —the Coit Maur or 'Great Wood' of Arthur's time—that clothed hundreds of acres of east Somerset, and parts of Wiltshire containing Bradford-on-Avon and Malmesbury. It created a name for the village of Penselwood. Outlaws and savages inhabited this forest so that travellers dreaded a journey through it, although tiny groups of wattle-and-daub huts had risen like colonies of drab mushrooms in clearings, not far from streams, hacked out by settlers still fierce and heathen. These settlements were the ancestors of various Somerset villages, now very pleasing to look on and sometimes set in beautiful landscape threaded by streams and small rivers. Selwood got its name from the 'sallows' or willows that fringed the numerous streams running out of it. Here, in Aldhelm's opinion, lay his mission-field where, as abbot or bishop, he personally undertook the task of summoning souls to God.

He made many journeys on foot from Sherborne, carrying his harp like a wandering minstrel. He would roam among the Selwood Forest settlements and attract the uncouth inhabitants by standing on a wooden bridge over their stream singing songs of his own composition and accompanying himself on the harp or lute. When his music had soothed the savage breasts of his listeners, he introduced sacred themes, and eventually allured the Saxon peasants to listen to his preaching and to receive the sacrament of baptism in their own familiar rivulet or sacred pagan spring.

An unclassified road turning off the noisy A303 in Wincanton, served also by the A372, leads to Cucklington that has one of the loveliest sites of all Somerset villages. Its houses, of which many are of old-gold stone roofed with brown tiles, cling to the hillside or stand on its summit with the church that is approached by a yellow gravel drive, crowned with a seventeenth-century belfry, and flanked by a barn of golden-brown stone. From the hilltop an immense panorama of woods, meadows, trees and farmland rolls away to Dorset. In spring the valley at the foot is rich with buttercups, cow-parsley, flowering hawthorns. When Aldhelm was in the Bruton district with his disciple-missionaries, he frequently travelled seven or eight miles to this beautiful place and preached to the inhabitants of its rude dwellings. He baptised his converts in the clear ice-cold spring gushing out of the hillside. The spring has long been called Babwell, which means St Barbara's Well (or spring); St Barbara, carrying her martyr's palm, is painted on a piece of medieval glass in the

33

church. Approached by a road on the left as one comes from the church, the spring is found opposite Babwell Farm; it provided Cucklington's drinking water for over a thousand years after Aldhelm's day. For all its ancient associations, it does not delight the eye; its water flows out of an ugly brickwork well-house under a grassy bank into a long brick-edged trough, where horses used to drink, then drips over a mossy lip into an iron grating.

Aldhelm and his band of missionaries built small churches of daub-and-wattle in the Selwood Forest clearings where his converts continued to worship. Saxon stone churches later replaced these primitive buildings. In a man-made clearing not far from a ford of the river Brue, that had its source in the depths of Selwood, at Bruton-in-Selwood—the modern Bruton—Aldhelm built a church that he dedicated to St Peter. It must have been of modest dimensions, but William of Malmesbury who saw it four centuries later described it as 'a large church called St Peter which was built and dedicated by the Holy Man with much care'.

Aldhelm set this church on an incline because the river Brue often flooded the land below, and afterwards persuaded King Ina to build—by about AD 690—a second, smaller church dedicated to the Virgin. This probably lay north of his own, the two occupying the elevated site where Bruton's present fifteenth century church reigns with impressive nobility over the delightful, haphazard composition of this little old town with its pink and ochre walls; the huddle of pink, brown, and grey tiled roofs; the covered passageways called bartons (a word peculiar to the district and used on place-name plates in Bruton), running transversely from street to street; and the fifteenth-century packhorse bridge of golden-grey stone patterned with grey and golden lichen, which is called Bow Bridge and listed as an ancient monument. Ina's church disappeared in about 1140, its dedication being added to that of Aldhelm's, and the present church is dedicated to St Mary alone. Today several busy roads pass close to the churchyard gates: the A308 to Wincanton, the A303 to Sparkford, the A359 to Yeovil, and the A371 to Shepton Mallet.

In the holiday season the sound of traffic fills the air as one stands on Church Bridge, where a chestnut-tree hangs over, and looks down on the shallow greenish water flowing over a bed of yellow stones. Here Aldhelm and his companions splashed through the ford to stand singing and preaching on a wooden bridge before baptising Saxon peasants—among them men who worshipped Thor, Woden and other fierce gods—with water from the spring that has long been called Patwell. Perhaps Aldhelm himself destroyed its pagan associations by consecrating it to St Patrick. Patwell is now disused; the locked-up square wellhouse, roofed with stone slabs and containing an old pump, stands at the north end of the bridge below the church.

At Bruton, Aldhelm built a mission-station, or rather a collection of hut-dwellings for his holy men, who went out from their community to perform spiritual labour among the people of the Selwood settlements. The legendary site of the mission-station is a beautiful one, if rather wet, but one has to envisage rough, incult ground and dense surrounding woodland, with a few little strips of cultivation, in place of the present valley fields and groups of trees. The A303 to Sparkford from Bruton church has an unclassified road marked 'Godminster' turning off it. Walking along this route you see fields plumed with trees on the right, and on the left the high, buttressed grey walls roped with ivy and the gabled dove-cote, in National Trust ownership, of the medieval abbey at Bruton. Further on, near woodlands, there is a grass-grown road leading to a farm and Godminster House where, in spring, the garden lawn is sheeted with snowdrops. Looking to the right, you will notice a narrow valley running through fields to a copse where fir trees grow; alders too are abundant because a little spring makes the ground swampy. This is Holy Water Copse and one of its neighbour fields is called Holy Fathers. In the solitude of this valley, Aldhelm's 'holy fathers' raised their huts of clay and wattle, and here the church has held a little procession in their memory. The grassy way up to Godminster House is private property but local people know field-paths to Holy Water Copse. According to a Bruton historian, Godminster has replaced the older name of Godmanstone.

Aldhelm came to another place cleared of the great forest trees, in a valley where a little river called the Frome ran towards the Avon. Summoned there by the reputation of its inhabitants for benighted savagery and ignorance of Christian virtues, he came with six monks to this settlement—often called Frome Selwood, now Frome (pronounced Froom)—arriving on Midsummer Eve. For Aldhelm and other Christians this meant St John's Eve, the day preceding the feast of St John the Baptist who preached in the wilderness and baptised believers in the river Jordan. Aldhelm found these forest-dwellers—particularly the people who lived in the vicinity of the place later called Woodlands, close to the Wiltshire border—even more wicked than he had expected, and was horrified to discover that they spent Sunday in brutal pastimes like badger-baiting and cock-fighting.

In the glorious dawn of Midsummer Day, Aldhelm took his stand with his six chosen men, all fired with the same zeal and faith, on a wooden bridge at the southern end of Frome, which today is a place of many bridges with the river winding in and out in the lower part of the town at the foot of steeply sloping streets into which little paved lanes drop like tributaries. The notes of Aldhelm's harp and the sound of men's voices raised in song called the curious peasants to the steep green banks of the Frome, to stare open-mouthed at the strangers, led by a tall man robed in white. The monks changed their songs to psalms, choosing those that offered joyous praise to God. Then Aldhelm preached with passionate eloquence, exhorting his listeners to reject their cruel pastimes and their grosser vices, and thus save their souls and be assured of the joys of Paradise. When he ended his sermon, a number came forward to be baptised and renounced the pagan rites they would have observed that midsummer night.

All that summer of AD 680, or thereabouts, the missionaries

won converts on the willow-fringed banks of the Frome and gave them Christian baptism. These new Christians, under Aldhelm's direction, built the first Christian church at Frome, erecting it on a hillside above the reach of the river. The site is occupied today by the parish church that has a wide paved courtyard with a five-arched gateway outside its west door. The church carries the dedication to St John the Baptist, that Aldhelm thought appropriate, and had been familiarly referred to as 'John of Frome'. Inside the church on its north side, among other saintly figures stands a statue of Aldhelm holding the model of a church. The brass plate beneath his sculptured image states: 'Saintly Aldhelm, Bishop of Sherborne, as tradition tells, laid the foundation of this sacred house about the year of our Lord 680'.

Two Saxon carvings are now built into the north-east wall inside the tower; though time has worn and defaced their design, it is still possible to make out an intricate knotwork pattern, a lion and the coils of dragons' tails. The smaller carving came from Aldhelm's Saxon church, which still stood in 1150, so William of Malmesbury recorded.

Later Aldhelm built a small monastery at Frome with its own little church. It depended on the Abbey of Malmesbury where Aldhelm was abbot. Not a fragment of the Frome monastery remains and there is nothing to point out its site; Danish marauders swept it away. But for years after Aldhelm's first visit, his mission-station carried on the work of converting the heathen of Selwood Forest. The woods at Longleat are a remnant of that savage wilderness. Aldhelm was remembered when the Church of England Waifs and Strays Society built St Aldhelm's Boys' Home at Frome.

This builder of churches and monasteries had a great love and knowledge of architecture as, despite late Saxon alterations, is testified by the church of St Lawrence at Bradford-on-Avon, not many miles out of Somerset. It belonged to the monastery Aldhelm built at Bradford where he baptised his converts in the Avon flowing below the church. Several of Aldhelm's churches

were replaced by churches built of stone from the quarries at
Doulting where tradition holds that Aldhelm was born, and
where he built a humble wooden church to serve his converts.

In this village, on the A361, one of Aldhelm's most interesting
places of baptism can be found, north of the church and in the
grounds of the former vicarage, now called Doulting Manor. It is
St Aldhelm's Well, which is really a spring gushing out under
two stone arches built against a natural rock face. Pieces of
dressed stone strewn on the ground indicate that a roofed building once stood over this source of the stream called Doulting
River or the Dulcote, that for many years supplied the village
with water and runs on to Shepton Mallet where at one time it
served the cloth-mills. Pilgrims who venerated the well because
of its connections with saintly Aldhelm used to bathe in the stone
trough that stood in front of the arches. Aldhelm himself once
performed the not uncommon saintly penance of sitting there in
the ice-cold water long enough to recite the whole of the psalter.
A *Gentleman's Magazine* drawing of the well shows that in the
eighteenth century a grotto of squared stones, 6ft high, contained
the water which flowed out over a low stone front between walls.
In the nineteenth century the water poured over in two jets.

Doulting church, one of the few—including the church at
Broadway, in Somerset—dedicated to St Aldhelm, is beautifully
situated behind an expanse of smooth green turf and flowing
branches of beech-trees growing near the headless stone cross
carved on its panels with the signs of the Passion. The stone
reredos in the church is carved with the full-length figures of six
saints, among whom is Aldhelm, seen on the far left next to
Dunstan with his blacksmith's tongs at his feet; close to Aldhelm
is the unusual sight of sculptured water pouring from the cleft of
a rock. Unhappily vandals recently knocked off the heads of these
six saints and so damaged the images that Aldhelm, carrying his
staff in his left hand, blesses the flowing water with a broken
right hand.

So for years he made his long expeditions to this part of his diocese, preaching, converting, baptising and building, besides carrying out his episcopal duties and directing the monks of his monasteries. He greatly loved trees and is said to have planted a number of ash trees all along his routes by the simple expedient of pushing into the soil an ashwood staff which he could make grow like St Joseph's hawthorn staff. These ash trees standing in various parishes were long called bishop's trees, the most famous example being a great ash tree at Bishopstrow, in Wiltshire, which has a church dedicated to Aldhelm. He was preaching there rather lengthily on a hot day and his audience grew inattentive. He struck his staff into the ground and they saw bark clothe the dry stick, which became sappy and threw out branches green with feathery young ash-leaves. The people shouted 'A miracle! a miracle!' Aldhelm answered that the tree was a gift from heaven and the place assumed the name Bishopstrow, bishop's tree. Perhaps another of Aldhelm's holy ash trees stood at Hallatrow in the Mendips.

Aldhelm found pleasure and relaxation in the music of his harp and in composing songs, both sacred and secular. King Alfred loved those songs two centuries later. Unhappily none of the verses Aldhelm wrote in Old English survive, but this rhyme in modern English is reputedly a metrical version of his rendering of Psalm 84:

> There the sparrow speeds her home
> And in time the turtles come;
> Safe their nestling young they rear,
> Lord of hosts, Thy altars near.

He supervised the making of a musical instrument that resembled an organ, the first of its kind ever seen in England: 'a mighty instrument of innumerable tones, blown with a bellows, enclosed in a gilded case'. St Dunstan read Aldhelm's account of its construction and felt inspired to make an organ himself at Glastonbury in the tenth century. Aldhelm gave his organ to his beloved abbey at Malmesbury, for he was eager to adorn his churches with precious objects, sometimes giving himself great trouble in transporting the treasures he acquired, particularly on the occasion of a visit to Rome when he determined to bring back to Somerset a white marble altar. This was an extremely heavy slab of Italian marble, 4ft long, 2¼ft wide, 1½ft thick, with a projecting rim beautifully sculptured in a pattern of crosses. The camel that was given the task of carrying the altar over the Alps, exhausted with the strain of bearing such a load, fell down, causing the marble to split into two pieces. By prayer and miraculous handling, Aldhelm mended the riven altar, so that it was marked only by a faint irregular scar on its surface; also by prayer he created renewed strength in the labouring camel which struggled on through the Alpine passes with its burden. Aldhelm triumphantly presented the marble altar to King Ina who, in accordance with the saintly bishop's known wishes, made a gift of it to the church of St Mary at Bruton, where the indefatigable William of Malmesbury admired it in 1115. There has been no glimpse of it for centuries. Aldhelm brought other valuable relics from Rome and gave them to the small church of St Michael that he had built at Bath.

Aldhelm believed that *black* marble must be used only in churches, and there generally for tombs. Such marble came from the Isle of Purbeck where Aldhelm visited the quarries. He declared that old pagan gods lived in some of the tunnels and bound them to stay there under the church's ban; but he ensured that a specially evil and potent god, who kept watch over *black* marble, could not harm the quarrymen if they hewed it for holy usage and no other.

Aldhelm, Bishop of Sherborne, widely renowned for his saintliness and intellectual attainment, went to Rome as the guest of Pope Sergius. He sang mass daily and, loving all beautiful and precious things, included among his vestments a scarlet silk chasuble exquisitely embroidered with a pattern of black scrolls enclosing peacocks. ('It is with us now', wrote William of Malmesbury.) Singing mass one day when sunlight streamed into the church, Aldhelm threw his chasuble behind his back where, through forgetfulness, nobody stood to receive it. Instead a broad ray of sunlight fell through the clear glass of a window and held the chasuble suspended without any hand touching it.

Even in old age Aldhelm stood tall and erect, with keen sight and hearing and a ruddy complexion. Up to his last days, when his strength failed a little, he remained active and continued travelling round the villages and churches of east Somerset. He visited the house of an extremely wealthy uncle named Kenred, who owned a score of manors, including Doulting, and who remained obstinately pagan although a close relative of Christian King Ina. On this visit, Aldhelm was attacked by sudden illness that he knew was mortal. Kenred's house stood close to the Roman Fosse Way, about a mile from Doulting, at the place now called Cannard's Grave, where the present inn still displays this unfestive name on its sign. One legend maintains that an older name was Kennard's (or Kenred's) *Grove* because Aldhelm induced Kenred to plant a grove of trees here beside the Roman road. Another insists that the name was Kenred's *Grave* owing to the fact that this pagan Saxon thane was buried here outside consecrated ground, with his horse and hound in the same grave.

Aldhelm considered it unfitting that a Christian bishop should die in a heathen household and ordered his attendants to carry him to the little church at Doulting, that he had built and always loved, and to lay him down on a stone slab inside. Here he died a few hours later, murmuring his last prayers. His departing spirit appeared to his friend Eigwin, Bishop of Wiccia (Worcester), requesting him to go at once to Doulting and ensure that Aldhelm's body was conveyed to Malmesbury.

With a cross carried before it, with tapers burning palely in the sunshine, with the joyous song of birds almost drowning the solemn chanting of clergy, and many of Aldhelm's converts kneeling in tears at the wayside or bringing sick relatives to be miraculously healed, the funeral procession wound its way through lanes transformed into green cloisters by the overhanging boughs of trees in glorious new leaf. It was early May in AD 709. The

41

journey was divided into seven stages, the procession resting at places where Aldhelm had built a church. The bishop ordered a stone cross to be set up as a memorial to the saint at every resting place.

These seven Saxon crosses were known for many years as bishop's stones, but came to be called the Aldhelm crosses. Several fragments of them came to light through the efforts of a modern Bishop of Bristol, Dr Forrest Browne. Frome was the first resting place and here, in the interior wall of the tower of St John's church, may be found part of the shaft of the Aldhelm cross, ornamented with sculptured beasts and an interlace pattern. In Bath Abbey, among the pieces of sculptured stone ranged on a wall of the choir vestry (the cloister), there are two fragments of Saxon crosses. One of these, no 9 in the display, is an excavated portion of the Bath cross associated with St Aldhelm, carved with an intricate interlace pattern. In Bath, the bearers of the saint's body set down the bier at Aldhelm's small church of St Michael, the now built-over site of which lay at the end of colonnaded Bath Street, close to where the old Cross Bath stands. This famous bath, which is still used and which in Aldhelm's time was a Saxon bathing pool that he could use for baptisms, may have got its name from Aldhelm's cross. A modern inscription tells the visitor that a cross was set up by a grateful Mary of Modena, James II's queen. But when Leland came there in the sixteenth century, he saw 'the Cross Bath, so called because it hath a Cross erected in the middle of it'.

At Bradford-on-Avon, eleven miles away, in the lovely little church of St Lawrence, with bushes of rosemary growing beside the door, a stone altar has been built with some of the Saxon stones that had been thrown down; above it there is a replica of a Saxon stone cross, in which are set two fragments of the Bradford 'Aldhelm Cross' sculptured with an interlace design.

Aldhelm's body was entombed at Malmesbury, but about the middle of the ninth century his bones were placed in a shrine, on the sides of which a Saxon artist depicted his five most famous miracles, including the legend of the Bruton altar and that of the scarlet chasuble.

Aldhelm was not often portrayed in the statuary or stained glass of Somerset churches, in spite of all his great work. His is probably the bishop's figure among those crowding the west front of Wells cathedral, whose right hand looks as though it held the model of a church. In the yellow-tinted glass in a window of Cothelstone church, near Taunton, he appears wearing his mitre and carrying a golden chalice. The inscription reads: St Aldhelm of Sherborne.

DUNSTAN

Saint and visionary; Abbot of Glastonbury and afterwards Archbishop of Canterbury; scholar, teacher, statesman, counsellor of kings; instigator of the Benedictine order in England; builder of the fourth church raised east of Joseph's wattle church at Glastonbury; artist, craftsman, calligraphist, musician, engineer, alchemist: Dustan grew up to be all these. He was the delicate, precocious child of the Saxon thane Heorstan, who lived at Baltonsborough—where the church is dedicated to St Dunstan—a few miles from Glastonbury. Some people think he was born at Edgarley, a hamlet on the Shepton Mallet road (A361), where, at the foot of the Tor and close to the present reservoir there stood, within living memory, a tumbledown barn made from a small ruined chapel dedicated to St Dunstan. For Baltonsborough, take the B3153 road that runs from Somerton to Castle Cary, turning left at a place called Christians' Cross, ignoring the first turn (to Barton St David) and taking the second turn, bearing left at Keinton Mandeville, past the Quarry Inn and houses built of the cold grey stone from local quarries. Soon, on the road between ploughed fields and wet pastures, evidence of the drainage work directed by Dunstan comes into view. The river Brue waters these lands and flows alongside stretches of the road, passing under a pretty stone bridge called Tootle Bridge. Here the Brue branches from its old bed and follows the course of the Southwood stream—this loops the hamlet of Southwood —because Dunstan diverted the water from its natural course. His straight two-mile length of river between Tootle Bridge and Baltonsborough is still called Dunstan's Dyke. The alternative name Bitterwater was also given to it, because a mile upstream a mineral spring flowed into it. He had the dyke cut to drain the swampy pastures on the edge of the Brue and to supply power to the mill—Baltonsborough Mill—that he built near the church. Until recent years an ancient mill was working on its site. His was the first waterwheel in this part of England, and supplying its power involved banking the stream for a long distance and making a weir at the place called Flights Weir, between Baltonsborough and the bridge. Right up to the twentieth century, Dunstan's engineering feat necessitated the lifting of hatches at Tootle Bridge every weekend to give water to the deprived and thirsty land at Barton St David.

At the fifteenth-century church, turn the iron door-handle finely wrought for it by a Baltonsborough smith, and look for No 117 among the new 'kneelers', which are catalogued with their subjects for the visitor's enlightenment. This vividly illustrates the oft-repeated legend of Dunstan working at his Glastonbury forge and resisting the Devil's wiles; Dunstan wears a vivid crimson gown. This story is portrayed in a number of stained-glass windows. At Cothelstone in the Quantocks, in the Stawell chapel of the little red sandstone church, there is a window in which Dunstan (named here as S. Dunstan de Glastonia), wearing a gown of yellow needlework and holding his metal-worker's tongs in his left hand, stands next to St Cuthbert. In Wells Cathedral, in a lower window on the south side of the south transept, the fifteenth-century glass portrays Dunstan, vested as an archbishop, gripping the Devil's nose with his tongs; but in the south window at St Martin's chapel he is more endearingly depicted giving a singing lesson to two princesses while an angel provides the harp accompaniment. He stands with two other saints in the third window on the south side of the choir clerestory, and in the south-east window of the Lady Chapel his head is seen next to Cuthbert's among a number of saintly heads on the lower tracery lights. It is unthinkable that he is not one of those sculptured bishops, too mutilated to be positively identified, that stand in magnificent array on the great west front of the cathedral. At Doulting, on the damaged stone reredos, he can be recognised because of the tongs lying at his feet. Naturally this illustrious Archbishop of Canterbury appears in the stained glass and sculpture of many churches outside Somerset. Stonyhurst at one time possessed a chasuble on which the Devil legend was embroidered. The Goldsmiths' Company took Dunstan, with his goldsmith's skill, for their patron and hung a painting of the legend in the Goldsmiths' Hall. A gilded wooden image of him stands there in a niche; it was the figurehead of the company's barge.

Legends began to accumulate round him even before he left his mother's womb. Heorstan and his wife, Kinedrida, who was pregnant, made part of a congregation worshipping in the church at Glastonbury on Candlemas Day AD 924 and holding lighted tapers. Suddenly every taper-light went out leaving Kinedrida's solitary taper burning so brightly that people marvelled as they relit their own from its flame, and accepted the event as a heavenly augury that the child she would bear 'would give light to all England'.

He was a gay, fair-haired little boy who enjoyed the company of guests in his father's hall and loved listening to their tales, to the songs that entertained them, and even more to the music of the harp. Yet this lively child soon fell under the power of religion. His parents took him very early to Glastonbury for schooling by the Irish scholars. On his first night there the excited boy lay unable to sleep, and had a vision of a man in white who took him by the hand and led him not only round Glastonbury's shrines and holy places, many of them in semi-ruin after Danish ravages, but through long pillared aisles and along ranges of monastic buildings enclosing a courtyard. None of these last had been created, but before his death in 988 Dunstan had started

45

raising them.

The Irish monks and pilgrims fascinated the imaginative child with their tales of saints and miracles, as well as with Irish songs sung to the harp. All the same he studied hard, too hard, so that he fell ill with a fever and they thought him dying. Yet he got out of bed and walked in a trance to the Abbey church where he found the great door locked. He gained entrance by a small door left unlocked by workmen, climbed up a mason's ladder till he reached the roof beams, walked lightly along them and dropped softly as a feather to the stone pavement of the aisle, quite unhurt because, so he told the awed monks who tenderly gathered up this sleepwalking child, an angel had commanded him to rise from his bed and had borne him from the roof on his wings when fiends would have thrown them down. From that night Dunstan became obsessed by the idea of the Devil's dreadful haunting presence.

He went to stay with his uncle Alphage, Bishop of Winchester, who was born at Weston, near Bath, and became Abbot of Bath Abbey. Alphage longed to win him for the church, but Dunstan loved a girl and resisted his uncle's persuasions. The intense mental struggle caused another attack of delirium, and on recovery he decided that his love for a woman was the most powerful temptation with which the Devil had assailed him. He rode back to Glastonbury fervent for religion, with his great joy in life quenched.

At Glastonbury his close friend Wulfrid died and appeared to Dunstan in a dream, indicating a place south of the church that within three days would be a monk's burial-place. Dunstan swore that he would take vows of monkhood if he 'dreamed true'. Before three days elapsed a monk died and was buried in a place he had requested in his last moments—the place in Dunstan's dream.

Dunstan adopted an extremely rigorous existence, but did not entirely deprive himself of the pleasure of feminine society. As spiritual counsellor to Ethelfleda, a widowed lady of wealth and high birth, he went often to her house west of the abbey. King

Athelstan and some of his court came as guests to the house and Ethelfleda, knowing that some years earlier jealous courtiers had alienated the king from Dunstan by asserting that he dealt in magic and cast spells, gave a feast at which she reconciled Dunstan and the king. Athelstan and his nobles drank very freely, the cup-bearers running back and forth so energetically that Ethelfleda feared her mead-casks must be nearly exhausted, but they were miraculously replenished, like the widow's cruse, because of Dunstan's presence.

Ethelfleda devoted almost all her wealth and time to religious work and spent hours with her maids embroidering vestments for the church. Dunstan, having created a design for them to embroider on a stole, sometimes played his harp to them, to lessen the tedium of long hours at such complicated needlework. One day he hung his harp on the wall so that he could minutely examine the lovely embroidery. Suddenly all of them sat motionless in silent wonderment as the harp sweetly played, without any touch, the antiphon *'Gaudent in coelis'*. Doubters of this miracle say that Dunstan made himself an Aeolian harp whose strings would respond to the movements of a breeze.

One evening as Dunstan made his way to vespers with some of his pupils he saw a pure white dove flying in the light of a spring sunset towards Ethelfleda's house and knew he had received a sign of her swiftly approaching death. She died within the hour and the loss was one of his heaviest sorrows for 'he clave to her and loved her'.

And now he mortified himself more intensely. He made himself an anchorite's cell too cramped for him to lie down at full length; it measured 5ft by 2½ft, and he could only stand upright in a central hole he had dug. This tomb-like place which joined the outer wall of the church was his oratory, dwelling and workshop, lit by a little window in its door which opened into the church.

Here he had his forge, hammer and anvil, and made fine articles of wrought iron. Here he made wonderful chalices, dishes and candlesticks of gold and silver. Here he performed an act that blazed his sanctity abroad, although the story is grotesque.

One grey evening as Dunstan worked at his forge and murmured his prayers, the Devil thrust his head through the window in the door and tempted the anchorite so seductively with tales of beautiful women and sensual delights that Dunstan found himself listening and not unwilling to be persuaded for he was in the flower of youth. With a swift movement he turned and seized the Devil's nose in the grip of his red-hot metalworker's tongs. Roaring with pain the Devil vanished, totally repulsed. This is the legend perpetuated in stained glass and religious paintings. Another version recounts that the Devil came as a beggar whining for porridge whereupon Dunstan, who had just made a silver ladle, used it to spoon a great helping of molten metal from his cauldron into the Devil's mouth. Others say that the Devil tempted him in the guise of a beautiful wanton woman who gained entrance to his cell and was frankly displaying her charms to seduce him when her nose was gripped by the cruel pincers.

A corner of Glastonbury Abbey ruins towards the east end, near the place where Dunstan's forge stood outside the north wall, is supposed to be haunted. If you lean your ear close to a hole in the masonry the 'blowing' noise of Dunstan's ghostly forge can be heard. But if the head of an abbot is ever seen there, as some assert, is it Dunstan's or that of the executed last abbot of Glastonbury?

After Edmund succeeded Athelstan as king, he came to his palace at Cheddar, below the southern scarp of Mendip, a mile distant from Cheddar Gorge. The site was excavated in 1960–2 before the building of the fittingly-named Kings of Wessex School, in the grounds of which the outlines of the palace buildings have been preserved. Edmund came here chiefly for the hunting in the dense forest that clothed the top of Mendip, where today the wind sweeps unimpeded over open stone-strewn country; but his Witan or council met here too, perhaps in the

60ft-long West Hall he built. Jealousy of the young, extremely gifted Glastonbury monk, who exercised such powerful influence over the king, led his nobles and counsellors to poison his mind against Dunstan, who was called to the Cheddar palace and angrily dismissed from Glastonbury. Dunstan returned in sorrow to the abbey and prepared to leave as an exile with a company of foreign scholars who were ending their visit.

Two days later the sound of hunting-horns and the baying of hounds echoed down the wild Cheddar Gorge as the king and his train hunted a stag through the forest-wilderness on Mendip. The king led the chase, urging his horse well ahead of his followers so that it galloped like the wind and was so excited that he had lost control of it when they broke abruptly from the forest. He saw the silhouetted antlered head of the great stag disappear over the red cliffs of the gorge in a tremendous leap that the hounds followed. The horse galloped on in mad excitement and Edmund saw his own death-leap ahead. In a flash he remembered his treatment of Dunstan and swore to make amends if God would save his life. On the brink of the cliffs his horse turned aside and quietened. Edmund motioned his alarmed nobles into silence and rode back to his palace without a word. 'God, thou hast preserved my life, I will be reconciled to thy servant.' He sent for Dunstan and rode back with him to Glastonbury where the abbacy was vacant, and on arrival took and reverently kissed Dunstan's hand, then led this young man of twenty-one to the abbot's chair and set him there.

'Be the ruler of this chair and its most powerful incumbent and the most faithful abbot of this church.'

During the three remaining years of Edmund's life Dunstan started rebuilding the half-ruined abbey and founding the great Benedictine establishment. When Edmund was cruelly murdered by an outlawed robber at a feast at Pucklechurch in Gloucestershire, they promptly sent for Dunstan. The messenger encountered him halfway, riding from Glastonbury to Pucklechurch, and aware of Edmund's murder because he had seen a small, mocking

49

D

devil dancing with delight in a beam of sunlight that filtered into his cell. Already Dunstan had ordered preparations to be made for the magnificent entombment of pious Edmund in the abbey church.

After King Edred died at Frome, Dunston, Abbot of Glastonbury, sat among the noblest guests at the coronation feast of dissolute King Edwy, who was so enslaved by his paramour that he left the feast for amorous dalliance. No one dared to seek him or to criticise this undignified conduct except Dunstan who reproached him in very candid terms. So strongly did he condemn the king's proposed marriage as incestuous that this time he found himself actually exiled to a foreign country, his wealth —some of it bequeathed by Ethelfleda—confiscated, even his friends punished. Again the Devil came at the hour of Dunstan's departure from his abbey to exult at his downfall, although only peal after peal of diabolical laughter thrown back in hollow echoes through the monastic buildings told Dunstan of his presence.

The exiled abbot turned his head and addressed his invisible enemy, 'Thou shalt have more sorrow at my return than thou hast joy at my departure'.

A year or two after the sixteen-year-old Edgar came to the throne, he made Dunstan, who had been recalled from exile, Archbishop of Canterbury. Yet for seven years Dunstan refused to crown him because Edgar had abducted 'a veiled lady' from a convent—that is, a girl of high family brought up by nuns and escaping in a nun's head-dress. Dunstan called the king an enemy of God and imposed long penance. Finally he crowned Edgar, married by that time to the beautiful, scheming Elgiva who hated Dunstan. The coronation took place in Bath, in the church dedicated to St Peter, on the present abbey site, in a setting of the utmost splendour. Nobles and churchmen assembled in the church, and the streets filled with a jubilant crowd in the dazzling sunlight of Whit Sunday 973. Its millenary was celebrated in Bath Abbey in May 1973. A tablet outside the abbey walls commemorates this unique Somerset coronation that was remembered during six centuries, when every Whitsuntide a 'king' was elected and feasted with his friends by rich Bath citizens. Edgar's coronation laid the basis of the ceremony used for the crowning of all English monarchs. The antiphon 'Zadok the Priest' was sung. The Archbishop of York assisted Dunstan, a sign that all England had united under young King Edgar, and to mark this significant event a stone cross was set up near the abbey. During modern excavations of the Roman baths, a portion of this cross of Northumbrian pattern was discovered and is now displayed (No 19) in the choir vestry, with the Aldhelm cross.

The 'Edgar window' in the abbey, which commemorates this coronation, portrays Dunstan CANTAB ARCHIEPISCOPUS in scarlet and gold. A third of its glass was destroyed in the blitz during the Second World War, but restoration was skilfully performed.

One day, not long after Dunstan's return from exile, King Edgar and he sat together at dinner in the refectory at Glastonbury, close to the great wooden crucifix hanging on the wall. Edgar was pondering over a secret plan to transfer the monks and to institute a mint at Glastonbury, while Dunstan ate in silence. Suddenly the wooden figure of the crucified Christ trembled from head to foot and shook the jewelled diadem that adorned its head to the floor, between king and abbot. Edgar crossed himself in fear and afterwards made full confession to Dunstan, accepted stern rebuke and penance, and abandoned his scheme.

Few legends of Dunstan reveal the geniality and liveliness that his biographers say were among his qualities, but one small homespun tradition certainly brings him down to more earthly things. It must have been invented by Somerset farmers a long time after his death to explain why frosts and cutting east winds sometimes prevail in mid-May, when such weather can blight the apple-blossom and ruin the cider-apple crop. Dunstan, they say, was an expert brewer of ale from barley and once struck a small bargain with the Devil who promised in return to blight the blossom of the fruit that made a rival beverage. Dunstan stipulated that the blighting must be restricted to the three days 17-19 May. Cider-makers, therefore, have always feared for their blossom around St Dunstan's Day, 19 May, and scan the sunset sky anxiously for premonitory signs of frost.

The archbishop was buried at Canterbury, which the Danes burnt about twenty years later. Glastonbury monks obtained royal permission to take Dunstan's venerated bones from the ruined tomb and bring them back to Glastonbury. In sight of home they set down their burden and rested at the place still called Havyatt—the name denotes a gate—which makes a gap in the strange small earthwork, Ponter's Ball, set astride the road east of Glastonbury, between Edgarley and West Pennard. The abbey bells, untouched by human hands, suddenly began to peal with a startling joy to celebrate the return of the saint, and the monks came running from their refectory to meet the cortège at Havyatt before any news had reached them. Some years later the plundering Danes turned back at Havyatt, except for a few who charged on through the Havyatt gap and were smitten with blindness. The cortège may have rested at Edgarley also, on the spot where a chapel to St Dunstan was built.

They laid his coffin beneath the pavement of King Ina's great church (to which Dunstan had added aisles and a tower), near the holy-water stone on the right of the entrance. Only two monks knew the exact place for fear that Canterbury would later reclaim such treasured relics, and until 1184, when most of the abbey buildings perished in the disastrous fire, the secret was passed on by some aged monk on his deathbed. After the catastrophe the monks made an intensive search among the ruins so as to retrieve all sacred relics that made Glastonbury a place of pilgrimage. When they lifted a pavement-stone in the church and found a coffin, word ran round that it might be Dunstan's. The monks assembled with the prior and watched the opening of the coffin. Inside it was painted half red, half blue and inscribed with the letters S D. Among the bones decked with jewels lay a finger-bone that wore the pastoral ring. There was no doubt. They placed the bones in a shrine of gold and silver, and set it in a chapel dedicated to St Dunstan. Until the Dissolution the Glastonbury shrine drew rich offerings from pilgrims attracted to it for healing and penitence.

A later Archbishop of Canterbury said that *his* monks had found Dunstan's coffin absolutely intact at Canterbury, with this inscription on a leaden plate:

HIC REQUIESCIT SANCTUS DUNSTANUS
ARCHIEPISCOPUS

Abbot Bere replied that 'a few bones' might have remained at Canterbury.

It was long remembered that Dunstan had a knowledge of alchemy, and in the reign of Queen Elizabeth, Dr Dee, that strange Renaissance scholar, mathematician, sorcerer, alchemist, and his companion, Kelly, had a search made in Dunstan's desecrated shrine. They found, so they said, two phials, one holding an elixir, 'the powder of projection', and manuscript instructions for transmuting mercury into gold, the magical science they longed to master. When installed at the court of Rudolph II in far Bohemia, Dr Dee claimed that he had made an ounce or two of gold by using the materials found among the bones of one of the greatest saints in Christendom. He had paid one guinea for them.

Dunstan's name has been attached with no definite reason to various Somerset bridges, wells and gates. St Joseph's Well, in the crypt of the Lady Chapel at Glastonbury Abbey, has alternatively been called St Dunstan's. One of the most beautiful and interesting places associated with him—none knows why—lies in a remote corner of Mendip in the tiny hamlet of Stoke Bottom. This is part of the parish of Stoke Lane or Stoke St Michael, a village answering to two names, four miles north-east of Shepton Mallet (A361). By the Oakhill Inn at the village of Oakhill, a signpost points to Stoke St Michael, and after following this road one must turn left towards Nettlebridge. This is a wide road yet so green and empty, its verges and banks so rich with campions and cow-parsley, with white Solomon's seal growing by the ditches and trees hung with ivy casting their shade, that one would not dream it had ever led to a coal-mining district. Silver birches border a field where a ribbon of bluebells threads a hedge-bank. After crossing a little stone bridge over the river Frome one descends a steep lane to the 'Bottom'. This is a lane even more green and lonely, in spring full of lacy cow-parsley, pink campions, pink and white hawthorn, with many singing birds in its trees. The floor of the woodlands on the left is whitened by and, redolent of, flowering garlic which hides a stream running to join the river in the Bottom. This bowl at the valley's end once held a busy paper-mill and a large number of cottages for the mill-workers. Now there is one house and a farm-house, Stoke Farm, high on the right behind a garden walled with Doulting stone; below this garden the Frome runs fast and sends its water pouring over the rocks to fall into Dunstan's well, which is a large round pool, ringed with buttercups and overhung by a white chestnut-tree.

Did the saintly abbot ever seek this place for a spell of contemplation?

2

Kings

BLADUD

For every thousand persons familiar with the name of King Lear, hardly one has heard of his father Bladud. Unless he lives in Bath. This beautiful city traces its ancestry back to the township King Bladud founded round the hot springs centuries before the Romans came; although Georgian Bath resembles its ancestors even less than the majestic oak resembles the acorn with which Bladud is so strongly connected. It does, however, bear imprints of Bladud's existence. The visitor entering Bath from the London road (A4) sees Bladud Buildings, stretching from the summit of steep Broad Street to join the curve of the Paragon. They are noticeable on account of a red chaise-longue set behind the wrought-iron parapet over an upholsterer's shop close to a corner known at one time as Chaise Longue Corner. In the nineteenth century the Bladud Bank occupied No 2, distinguishable by a carved wooden bust of Bladud that was set outside the building no later than the 1790s. This bank passed to

Stuckey's, which merged with the Westminster Bank, in whose Milsom Street premises this crowned head of Bladud looks down benignly from a plinth inside the main hall. It is a strange, skilfully carved representation, almost certainly by Grinling Gibbons, who gave him a serene, refined face with the trim Van Dyck beard and pointed lace collar of a seventeenth-century gentleman. If one walks on to the Pump Room and looks out of the middle window one will see an image of Bladud executed with a little more verisimilitude, a crowned, robed figure holding a sceptre and set in a niche in the far wall behind the King's Bath. This is the figure Rowlandson drew; and in the drawing by Thomas Johnson, as early as 1672, the inscribed tablet reads:

> Bladud, son to Lud Hudibras,
> The eighth King of the Britains [sic]
> From Brute: a Great Philosopher
> And Mathematician: bred at Athens
> And Recorded the First Discoverer
> And Founder of these Bathes, Eight
> Hundred Sixty and Three yeares
> Before Christ, that is Two thousand
> Five Hundred Thirty Five Years
> SINCE
> ANNO DOMINI 1672

In the nineteenth century another figure of Bladud—life size, and carrying a staff—stood by the Mineral Water Drinking Fountain (hot water) in Stall Street. When the city authorities removed it, the owner of a house in Entry Hill, off the Bath–Wells road, bought it for his garden and renamed his house Bladud Villa. Just before World War II this figure stood looking into the fishpond of another Entry Hill garden.

Lud Hudibras, King of Britain, held his court somewhere near Stonehenge. He had one son, handsome and talented, named Bladud, who fell a victim to leprosy in the full flower of his youth. The king's panic-stricken subjects petitioned for Bladud's removal so that Hudibras had no choice but to banish him. The weeping queen did not dare approach her son as she uttered her farewells, but took from her finger a ring of intricately-chased gold, laid it on the ground and told Bladud to keep it so that if he were restored, even many years later, he might show it her as proof of his identity. So he departed, on a wandering course along chalky tracks over the open downlands, eating berries and any birds or hares he could snare. No one would give him work or even food, since an obviously runaway boy in rich soiled clothes awoke suspicion, until he managed to obtain a ragged smock and hose from a shepherd lad. He wandered for miles begging his bread, until he reached a district, near the place now called Keynsham, where the little river Chew runs into the wider Avon, roughly halfway between Bath and Bristol.

At that time the region was covered by acres of massive oak-woods whose branches dropped a plentiful acorn harvest for the swine. Not for hundreds of years would the Romans build their villas with the tessellated pavements that have been uncovered there, nor the lofty-towered Christian church rise to dominate the straggling town-street along the Bath–Bristol road, nor the Norman abbey buildings appear nor the houses now surrounded by suburbia. Venomous snakes abounded in the forests; centuries must pass before St Keyna would leave her royal home in Breck-nock to live in this wild place (named after her) as a holy virginal recluse, charming the snakes with Christian prayers that turned them into the 'snake-stones' or 'Keyna's stones', the curled am-monites found in quarries and set in many Keynsham walls.

Here, an old swineherd gave Bladud work as a swineherd's boy. He drove his herds of swine deeper into the forest to feed on acorns, and they flourished—until they caught his own disease and became scaly and sickly. Fearing his employer's wrath he hid himself even further inside the oak forest, feeding his herds on the plentiful acorns. Then one day they came to a spot where the sparkling Avon shallowed to make a ford and, as the acorns lay strewn more thickly on the far bank, he drove his swine over the water to feed. The crossing place later received the name of Swineford and kept it till this day. The Avon still runs shallow there below the houses.

After driving his swine for several miles Bladud settled with them in the deep bowl of a valley whose slopes were clothed with oaks. The massive height of Solsbury Hill towered over his resting-place that, according to tradition, came to be called Swineswick (tellers of legendary tales take little account of etymology), now the village of Upper Swainswick. Here Bladud set up pens or cribs for his swine to occupy at night; daily he drove them to feed in the woods; daily they grew more sickly and diseased, while his own malady worsened. One morning after opening the cribs he turned to worship his chief deity, the rising sun, and as he did so saw his swine rush like mad creatures along the riverside valley until he lost them. It took several hours' wandering to find them. They had discovered a warm swamp matted with rotting leaves and vegetation, and here they wallowed joyfully. When they emerged they were plastered with hot mud. Bladud washed this away and it seemed to him that some of the leprous scales had disappeared.

On succeeding days he let them wallow for hours in the warm morass, which they would leave only when he coaxed them away by walking ahead scattering acorns from his satchel. Centuries later, Bladud luring his swine with acorns was sculptured over bronze doors of the Roman baths. Afterwards he would wash them and pen them in a state of cleanliness. Finally their leprosy vanished.

Suddenly he thought of trying the same treatment and bathed daily in the warm mud, that he observed was created by hot springs bubbling from the ground and covered with a growth of aquatic plants; finally he was cured. Filled with joy he drove the swine back to the old swineherd, whom he persuaded to believe his incredible story and to accompany him to his father's court.

They found Hudibras and his queen holding a feast, to which a ragged old swineherd and his sunburnt boy could not be admitted. Bladud persuaded a servant to drop into the queen's wine-cup the chased gold ring that he always carried on a cord about his neck. The queen drained her wine and saw the ring's glitter.

'Bladud my child! Where is he?' she cried down the hall.

So Bladud came home amid great rejoicing.

After a while he persuaded Hudibras to let him go to Greece where he attained great learning in mathematics, philosophy and necromancy. Eleven years later he succeeded to his father's crown, but abandoned the place of Hudribras' court and returned to the neighbourhood of the bubbling hot springs that had cured his leprosy. Around them he built a township he called Caerbadon, that would become the city of Bath. He dedicated the curative springs to a goddess called Sul, so that the Romans later named his town Aquae Sulis and the great protective hill hanging over the north side of Bath came to be known as Solisbury or Solsbury. On this hill he raised a temple to Apollo whom the Greeks had taught him to worship.

He had learned other things from the Greeks. They had inculcated so keen an interest in scientific experiment that Bladud fashioned himself a pair of wings and made an experimental flight from a pinnacle of Apollo's temple on the summit of Solsbury. He soared skywards until, on failing wings, he crashed to his death on the temple high above his city, where he had built his palace on ground now in Manvers Street between Bath Spa station and the present Baptist church. Centuries had still to elapse before the top of Solsbury turned into a great walled camp full of timber-and-wattle buildings.

There are those who reject the story of the swine and believe that Bladud himself created the hot springs by the arts of necromancy. At a great depth in the Bath earth, he is said to have buried two tuns of burning brass and two others made of glass, filled with salt and brimstone. These, placed over the water-springs, fermented and produced great heat that kept them boiling. He set up cisterns near the springs.

Alternatively he is credited with being a magician in league with the Devil, so that he mysteriously heated the springs by laying in them a hot stone 'big as a tree'. In spite of these black arts, the curative effect of the hot springs attracted hundreds of the sick for healing. Bladud placed the waters under the guardianship of Sul—Minerva—and kindled his magic fires in her temple, where they were never quenched, never turned to ash, but finally turned to balls of stone.

Upper Swainswick village lies three miles north-east of Bath, off the A46, in the untouched bowl-shaped valley rimmed by lofty hills whence the high winds come sweeping to roar in the churchyard trees among the ivied tombs of yellow-grey stone. John Wood the elder, who created so much of Georgian Bath, lies buried in this church, as he specially desired because he so firmly adhered to the Bladud legend. One wonders why the resting-place of this famous man is so regrettably hidden under the small organ in the chapel of the north aisle.

At lower Swainswick, among the little spinneys now falling before building development, the old inn called the Bladud Arms still stands for the time being opposite the old toll-cottage. In the nineteenth century a cold mineral spring created a tiny spa here, called Bladud Spa, as well as a Spa Garden; this mysterious spring disappeared, reappeared, then got lost.

Through Bladud the city of Bath remained linked with the village of Swainswick. In the seventeenth century the handsome stone manor-house north of Swainswick church belonged to the Prynne family, of which the Cromwellian Prynne was a member. During the rebuilding of their tithe barn a sword was discovered in the collar-beam roof; it was cherished at the house as a family treasure for many years, to be displayed to such interested travellers as the parson-historian Collinson, who was scornful of people credulous enough to call it Bladud's Sword. However, it was known as Bladud's Sword, sometimes the Swainswick Sword, for over two-and-a-half centuries, during which it was carried at the head of all civic processions in Bath, from the reign of Charles I when a Prynne was Recorder. The sword, measuring

5ft 4in, is two-handled, with the arms of Bath blazoned on its blade; it bears the date 1423 and the initials R. D. When found it was encased in a worn scabbard of ribbed leather. The Bladud sword is now owned by Oriel College, Oxford, but a fine replica of it is used in Bath civic processions.

Bladud did not forget the swineherd who employed him when he found himself an outcast. He gave the old man a house, herds of swine and lands at a place that became the village Norton Malreward. The old swineherd lived in the district that is called Hog's Norton for reasons that many consider obvious.

ARTHUR

Somerset people, and many outside the county, hold the firm conviction that Arthur belongs to Somerset, whether their image of him is the chivalrous king with his train of knights, decked in the verbal embroideries of Malory and Tennyson, or the more realistic sixth-century British chieftain who over many years skil-fully led men of western Britain to repel the heathen Saxon invaders until he met his death at the Battle of Camlann

and the last lights flickered out,
And men in darkness murmured: Arthur is gone.

In Cornwall, Wales and Scotland, he was born, fought many battles and married Guinevere. The marriage ceremony was per-formed at Caerleon by Saint Dubricius, who founded a church at Porlock in West Somerset, where the present church is dedicated to him, and where, above Porlock Hill, two great stones called the Whitstones have lain horizontally in a bed of heather ever since the saint and the Devil held a hurling contest on Hurlstone Point across the bay. But it was in Somerset, according to its legends, that Arthur dedicated himself to the service of Christ and the Virgin; kept his court or stronghold; fought his twelfth and greatest battle; fought his last; received his fatal wound; cast away his sword Excalibur; was borne to the region called Avalon or Isle of Apples for healing; died there and was buried in most sacred ground at Ynyswitrin, now Glastonbury. Alternatively, the dying Arthur was carried in a boat over the waters of a great mere near Ynyswitrin towards a more mystic Avalon, the Celtic paradise beautified by trees bearing golden apples, whence Arthur will come again.

In Arthur's youth, when he ruled the country round Dunster in West Somerset in alliance with a chieftain called Cadwy, the local inhabitants implored his help against a dragon which ravaged the countryside round Dunster and the adjacent villages of Carhampton and Old Cleeve. At that time the region was a huge marsh interrupted by dense woodland and bounded by blue-grey and yellowish cliffs that reared above a brown rock-strewn shore and the grey waters of the Severn Sea. Arthur hunted the dragon, following its tracks for miles over the marsh and down to the rough shore until he saw it swimming far out at sea. The peasants had told him that even the most fearless hunters were helpless against this monster which ravaged crops, devoured beasts and herdsmen, and carried off children. As Arthur watched the serpentine creature coiling in the waves, he noticed a square stone object floating towards him. When the tide cast it up on the grey-brown shingle, he saw that this piece of stone was striated with beautiful colours and when he picked it up recognised it in amazement as a portable altar. He carried it away for his own use but learnt next day that a strange man, wearing a sheepskin and carrying an ashen staff, was wandering around asking the peasants if they had seen a small altar washed up by the sea. The little man had made several journeys down to the shore and returned burdened with large stones that he heaped up in a lonely place on the marsh, saying he meant to build an oratory and set his altar in it. He told them his name was Carantoc.

This man was heir to the kingdom of Ceredigion in Wales (the modern Cardigan), but as he desired to renounce all earthly riches he had run away from his father's court, put on a shepherd-boy's sheepskin and crossed the Severn Sea, casting his portable altar out of the boat and into the waters so that God should reveal the place where he must set it up. He came ashore on the outskirts of the Carhampton marsh and sat down under a tree waiting for a divine sign to direct his actions. As he meditated, he started making a staff from a rod of ash cut in the woodland, whittling away the rougher part with his knife so that shavings strewed the ground.

A wood-pigeon swooped and carried off a wood-chip in its beak. Having watched the pigeon's flight, Carantoc set off in the same direction across the marsh. When he picked up the shaving he recognised the sign from God and started to build a rough stone oratory that in later years was replaced by the Chapel of St Carantoc. The marshy district where this oratory stood was called Carrum—a place among rocks.

Arthur encountered this holy man near the shore and, when Carantoc asked if he had seen an altar cast up by the sea, replied that he would yield it up if the saint recompensed him. Carantoc asked what payment was required and Arthur pointed to the huge coiling dragon swimming in the sea. He told him how Carrum had been devastated, and said: 'If you are the Lord's servant rid the people of this monster and your altar shall be restored to you.'

Carantoc knelt to pray on the stony shore, then waded into the sea and called the dragon across the waters. The monster swam obediently towards him and uttered a gentle, welcoming cry. When it came close, the saint threw his scarf about the great scaly neck, that it encircled with difficulty, and the dragon 'used no wing nor claw' but let the saint lead him, docile as a lamb, across the marshes into Cadwy's citadel on the height now crowned by Dunster castle. He stood, quiet and friendly, on the rush-strewn floor of the hall while people forgot their terror and crowded round him. The saint forbade them to kill the dragon, commanded him to do no more harm and sent him out through the gates to live peaceably in some lonely place away from men's dwellings. Then Arthur yielded the altar, which Carantoc placed in his little stone oratory, and gave him perpetual possession of the land called Carrum. This is now Carhampton, on the A39 a few miles from Minehead.

A Chapel of St Carantoc—whose feast day is 16 May—stood on the oratory site for several centuries and served as the parish church as late, it appears, as Edward II's reign. By 1300 two churches were in existence, the second dedicated to St John the Baptist, as is the present church, which was rebuilt in Victorian times but is worth a visit for the sake of its lovely painted fan-vaulted screen of the fifteenth century. Leland saw the Chapel of St Carantoc in its last days. Its likely site—that is, the place where Carantoc raised his oratory—is the garden, or the orch-ards adjoining, of the former vicarage at Carhampton, the big square house of red sandstone east of the present church. In 1828 workmen dug up many stones from this ground and found a line of skeletons that seemed to indicate a churchyard.

A year or two after Arthur returned the altar to him, an angelic voice ordered St Carantoc to cast it once more into the sea. He obeyed, and this time the sea washed it up at the mouth of the river Guellit. On land near the river-mouth, bestowed by Arthur, Carantoc founded a little monastery or 'civitas' named Carrov, where he settled several holy men and performed many acts of healing before the heavenly voice called him to take up his altar 'of wonderful colour' and sail away to Ireland.

The Guellit was later called the Willett. In Carantoc's time it ran unsullied from its source near Elworthy high in the Brendon Hills, where a tower called Willett Folly is a conspicuous feature, through fields where Williton would be built, and down to the sea at Doniford, near Watchet. The modern map-name for the final stretch of this river, between Sampford Brett and Doniford, is Doniford Stream.

Doniford is reached by taking the unclassified road to Watchet off the A39 at St Audries. The field close to the sea, beyond the stone bridge with pebbles from the shore set in its coping, could be the ground Arthur gave Carantoc for his little city of Carrov. His hermits could look across to the blue mound of Steep Holm, and the long blue streak of Flat Holm, rising from the water. The Doniford Stream rushes fast and noisy, green with tree-reflections, from under the bridge to flow across the field past the deserted army camp towards the stony shore. For the last part of its course it is named the Swill.

Between Glastonbury and Burnham-on-Sea, cone-shaped Brent Knoll rises like a green citadel from the huge pastoral plain of central Somerset. Citadel it has been since before Arthur's time, bearing on its crest a fortified oval camp supplied by a plentiful spring and displaying on its flanks a pattern of ramparts. The Romans called it Mons Ranarum, or the Mount of Frogs, which name remained in local use until modern times and appropriately described it during the centuries when the plain encompassing the hill was a tract of constantly-flooding marsh.

In Arthur's time, according to legend, three giants, fierce as ogres, occupied the fortress and, when they saw travellers on the causeway, sallied down to murder them. At Caerleon for the Feast of the Nativity, Arthur knighted a brave young prince called Ider, who afterwards accompanied Arthur's fighting-company into Somerset. To test his valour Arthur commanded him to ride ahead and do battle with the giants on the Mount of Frogs. Ider accepted the task and rode boldly over the plain towards the hill while Arthur delayed long enough for Ider to prove his prowess. When Arthur arrived the young knight lay dead on the steep hillside near the corpses of the three slain ogres, while his horse cropped the grass. In great remorse Arthur hastened to Ynyswitrin a few miles away, appointed monks to say masses for Ider's soul and gave Brent Knoll and the lands of Brent Marsh, as well as precious chalices, to the monastery. The digging-up of an ancient cuirass, very heavy and of seemingly Roman craftsmanship, which was found near the village of

65

E

East Brent early in the nineteenth century, gave new colour to the story.

At one time Arthur—in rebellion against his overlord King Melvas, who ruled the *aestiva regio*, or Summer Kingdom, the land now called Somerset—lived mainly in Cornwall and Devon, where Melvas's forces frequently attacked him and his company of trained followers. Melvas treacherously seduced Arthur's wife, faithless golden-haired Guinevere, and carried her away to live with him as his paramour. By the time Arthur had raised levies in Cornwall and Devon, he had lost trace of Melvas's flight and nearly a year passed before the two armies confronted each other near the queen's hiding-place. Melvas kept his court in a lofty stronghold at Ynyswitrin protected from attack by acres of peaty bogland, by meres, pools and rivers that spilled over into floods, by great beds of reeds and thickets of alder. This city stood on the Tor in the place where, three centuries earlier, the Fairy King Gwyn ap Nudd had held his gay court in a castle, to which little St Collen had valiantly climbed from his cell at the foot, bearing his vessel of holy water for rites of exorcism. Collen resisted the wiles of the fairy maidens; threatened the mocking fairy people, in their gowns of blue and red, with the blue ice and red fires of hell; sprinkled them, and the king, his throne of gold and the glassy walls, with holy water, so that the castle and its fairy inhabitants vanished like hill-mist and the empty top of the Tor showed itself clothed in shivering grasses.

Now, as two armies threatened bloodshed for the sake of a wanton woman, another saint intervened. Gildas, rightly nicknamed 'the querulous' on account of his sour face and perpetual complaints, had lived for years as a fiercely ascetic anchorite on the rocky, barren island of Steep Holm in the Severn Sea, with only gulls' eggs and shellfish for his sustenance. When pirates from Orkney drove him out he set sail for Ynyswitrin, where the abbot received him cordially and allowed this great scholar the use of the famous library of manuscripts for writing his history

66

of British kings.

Now Gildas, stern and upbraiding, walked through the armoured hosts and mediated between Melvas and Arthur. He persuaded Melvas to yield up Guinevere to her husband—perhaps with reminders of eternal punishment—and Arthur, whom he personally disliked as a rebel, to swear brotherhood with Melvas. Guinevere departed obediently with her husband. Gildas eventually returned to a hermit life and built himself a cell and chapel, dedicated to the Holy Trinity, by a stream near the site of the present church at Street, not far from Glastonbury.

High up on Wirral Hill, not far from the Holy Thorn, stood a convent of nuns dedicated to St Peter. Here Arthur sometimes rested on his way to Camelot, enjoying the sweet tranquillity of the place, and within these walls a strange dream disturbed him. An angel's voice pierced his sleep, bidding him rise at daybreak to go to the hermitage of St Mary Magdalene on the green knoll called Beckery in the ever-flooding marshes west of Glastonbury. In the previous century Bridget—the young Irish saint whose mother's birth-pangs started while she was milking the cow so that her pitcher of milk spilt over the new-born child—had spent several years on this raised islet, leaving her scrip, rosary, hand-bell and weaving-combs behind at her departure, so that the oratory became a place of pilgrimage. Pilgrims used a paved ford over the river Brue at the westernmost end of the island. In the Middle Ages the figure of Bridget milking a cow—she was known to increase the yield of butter for dairymaids—was sculptured on the tower of St Michael's church on the Tor, where one still sees it, and a chapel to St Bridget—not the first—was built where the old oratory had stood. During a very hot summer in the 1880s, lines visible on parched grass on the highest part of Beckery seemed to indicate the site, and modern excavations have confirmed this evidence. In the early years of this century, a bronze bell, called St Bridget's, was shown in Glastonbury; it resembled the hand-bells of early Celtic missionaries that can be seen in the National Museum of Wales.

Twice Arthur dismissed his dream. On the third night he confided it to his servant, telling him that he would heed it if it occurred again. The servant rose stealthily while Arthur slept, and by moonlight or lantern-light crossed the marshes to Beckery, entered the chapel and saw a man's body lying on a bier with four tapers burning at each side. Their flames revealed the gleam of gold candlesticks on the altar. He seized one, hid it under his cloak, and as he fled home, passed a darkly clad man who stepped in silence from the gloom and stabbed him in the groin.

He managed to reach his bed, where Arthur, hearing him groan, ran to listen to his gasped-out story. Arthur lifted the blanket, saw the gold candlestick and found the dagger still thrust in the man's body. When his servant died Arthur knew that he must undertake a solemn enterprise. In the grey dawn of Ash Wednesday he followed the Roman road along the back of Wirral and crossed the marshland to the isle of Beckery. He entered St Mary Magdalene's chapel, feeling the weight of his sins upon him, fell to his knees and humbly confessed them to the aged black-gowned priest of the chapel. While the priest vested for mass, Arthur saw the flickering taper-flames burning in the near darkness and made out the shape of the bier with a shrouded corpse on it. The body was that of a hermit who had been visiting the chapel and for whom the mass was intended. This hermit was a member of the holy fraternity whose rough cells were set on Andersey or Nyland, a hill rising from the moors near Cheddar and now part of a parish known as Nyland-cum-Batcombe.

Suddenly the chapel filled with glory. The Virgin appeared in radiance, carrying her Son whom she gave to the priest. He set the Child beside the chalice on the altar. When he recited 'Hoc est corpus meum' he raised the Child high and set him on the altar again. Instead of the host, Arthur received and consumed the divine Child who reappeared miraculously whole on the altar. Arthur stayed kneeling in awe as the Virgin approached to give him a crystal cross before she vanished with the Child in her arms. He vowed a lifetime of service to the Virgin and her Son, renouncing his partial allegiance to the old pagan gods, and assumed for his arms a silver cross on a green field, with the image of Mary carrying her Son on the right arm of the cross.

A similar image of the Virgin painted inside his shield protected Arthur through three days of slaughter, when, killing a huge number of the Saxon foe with his own weapons—chiefly his renowned sword Excalibur that had been forged at Ynyswitrin—he won his major victory at Mons Badonicus, or Mount Badon. The treacherous enemy had turned back from their homeward journey to sail up the Severn Sea and besiege Bath, the Romans' abandoned Aquae Sulis, a walled city covering about twenty acres, its bath-houses and temples lying ruined in the swampy valley below the towering, protective hill-camps. Arthur and his men, who had hastened back from Scotland, forced the Saxons in falling darkness to take their stand on Bannerdown. This hill, north-east of the present village of Batheaston, was traversed by the Roman Fosse Way running to join the Via Badonica that led into Wiltshire. At dawn on a summer day in AD 516 Arthur drove the enemy, who fought a ferocious rearguard action, across the valley from Bannerdown on to Solsbury Hill, north-west of Batheaston, where he overwhelmed them. In later centuries men reported that they had gathered 'caps full of men's teeth in following the plow on Bannerdown'. Vainly the Saxons sought refuge in the great camp on the Solsbury plateau, behind its ruined ramparts of stone, at one time twenty feet wide, that had been built and overthrown, like the timber-and-wattle huts inside, before the Christian era dawned. In 1936, this historic plateau was presented to the National Trust by Mrs Hicks of Batheaston. It commands marvellous views of Mendip, of Somerset and Wiltshire, looks down on Bath and the river Avon, that defended one side of the fort, and the pretty villages of Batheaston and Swainswick cradled among cornfields and meadows. Cattle graze its slopes, but purple thistles and sorrel flourish among the strewn yellow stones on the summit and chunks of stone project through the turf. From Fosse Lane in Batheaston, four miles east of Bath, the track curves steeply upward for a long distance between wild thick trees and bushes and a dark overhang of hedge. Some of its stones may have come from the camp's ruined ramparts.

On a hot still day an eerie atmosphere oppresses the pedestrian toiling up to the ancient place that saw Arthur in combat for the fair territory all around it; Bladud many centuries earlier; and worshippers of the British goddess Sul, whose name Solsbury commemorates.

After his victory, which gave western Britain a twenty-five year reprieve from Saxon rule, Arthur chose the high place above Wells, now called Arthur's Point and rather isolated by modern quarrying operations, as his lookout post. It rears over the entrance to the valley where the river Axe bursts from the confines of Wookey Hole cavern, home of the Witch of Wookey. She had turned to stone long centuries before Arthur's time, although one legend tells of Arthur fetching a Glastonbury monk to achieve this. The lookout commanded the sea-approaches and the mouths of the Brue, Parrett and Axe; as well as the nearly empty green valley, where Wells Cathedral would rise; the wide glistening mere near Glastonbury; and the Tor crowned perhaps by a Christian oratory, or by the small stronghold of Melvas or of some other chieftain.

By what name Arthur called his tremendous emerald-green fortress in south Somerset is not known; the Saxons named it Cadbury and men of a later age Camelot, which derived from the little river Cam (meaning crooked) that trickles out of Camel Hill. From the domed summit known as Arthur's Palace the stream looks like a silver cord strung across the fields of South Cadbury and Queen Camel, where it passes under a tiny packhorse bridge, and Sparkford—by the churchyard wall—to join the Yeo.

Like Arthur's sentries, one sees the flat plains of the former extensive marshlands, the Vale of Avalon, the misty Tor, and far horizons, jagged by Mendips and Blackdowns and hazy Quantocks beyond Sedgemoor. Under the ploughland and meadows made from acres of drained morass lies the British trackway, called Arthur's Hunting Causeway, which started near the fort's south-west entrance to run north-west to Glastonbury; it is now scarcely traceable although it served as a bridle-track early in the century. 'Arthur's Hunting Path', the old men called it, and on stormy winter nights it is said that Arthur and his companions can be heard galloping along the causeway towards Glastonbury with their hounds giving tongue. Traditionally, the hounds slake their thirst at Arthur's Well in the fourth fosse on the fort's eastern slope.

On Christmas Eve the ghostly company rides out of the camp and descends in another direction to the village of Sutton Montis below Cadbury, moving more slowly and sedately, for the slope is precipitous. They ride along the quiet road towards Sutton Montis church and let their horses drink from the stone-rimmed well that is now inside the orchard of Abbey House, really a medieval priest's house of Ham stone. People in Sutton Montis, including some who say they are not superstitious, have heard the chink of hooves, the ghostly jingle of a bridle, on some Christmas Eve when they lay awake. As the well is inside the orchard and now covered, the drinking-place could be the clear little runnel of water that issues between fronds of hart's tongue fern from a bank in the lane, filling a stone trough beneath it. It is fed by the same spring as the well.

On nights of the full moon the horsemen ride round the ramparts and their horses' shoes flash silver. Then they water the horses at Arthur's Well. Youths and girls used to come daringly to drink at the well, so that their dreams might come true, and carved their initials on the bark of some of the camp's many trees. St John's Eve held special magic. A true-hearted person who bathed his eyes in the well might see the hill open, and glimpse Arthur and his men sleeping a tranced sleep within, swords near at hand ready for the day when Arthur comes again. 'Have you come to take the king away?' an old man asked a visiting antiquary in 1902.

In Tudor times local people swore the plough had turned up a silver horse-shoe, and lovingly carried away bits of 'dusky blew' stone from the 'old ruins' inside the enclosure. Belief that the hill is hollow grew with the centuries. When the 20-acre enclosure was cultivated, a barley-stack near one of its entrances sank below the earthworks before it could be threshed. The clang of the stone lid of Arthur's Well echoes hollowly near Queen Anne's (St Anne's) Well on the other slope; and it was believed that if one were to dig deep enough one would find a hollow chamber storing a hoard of gold.

'Finds' multiply the legends. When a clergyman-antiquary once came upon a broken quern or hand-mill inside the camp, his gardener remembered that 'fairies' had often carried up small quantities of reaped corn from a field below the hilltop. If any old men survive whose great-grandfathers swore they had seen 'corners of iron doors' among the ash-trees growing in the fosses, they will surely feel triumphant that an iron bearing belonging to an iron gate turned up in recent excavations. What new legend of Arthur's queen may grow up around the silver brooch, decorated with a chip-carved animal-head, recently found near the south-west entrance? What tales of Arthur will emerge from the discovered remains of a huge feasting hall of Arthurian times and of formidable fortifications raised in his lifetime?

The whole character and appearance of this massive hill—'a very Torre wonderfully enstrengthened,' as Leland called it—nourish the belief that it served as court and fortress to the greatest of Dark Age chieftains: its size, its comparative inaccessibility, its four-deep concentric fosses, its huge ramparts cut into the rock, and its 20-acre enclosure.

To reach Cadbury Castle, turn off the A303 on to the road to South Cadbury and Sutton Montis; then walk up Castle Lane, a narrow, hedged track which begins its ascent near South

Cadbury church. Once known as Arthur's Lane, it is set with rough stones, often slippery with cowpats from the herd that comes down for milking at Castle Farm across the village street; and on each side the ferns, nettles and cow-parsley are abundant. Beyond a rickety field-gate at its end, a broader unpaved track, that is very muddy in wet weather, leads up through the green gloom of overhanging trees to the scarped slopes of Cadbury Castle and its main entrance.

Somewhere near the banks of the crooked river Cam the ageing Arthur fought his last heroic battle, Camlann. He received fatal wounds at the hands of his bastard son, the worst of which was visible in his skull several centuries later. Centuries later still, men who found a large number of male skeletons packed in trenches in the field called Westwoods, west of the camp, felt certain that they were some of Arthur's warriors buried after his last battle with the Saxons.

Arthur's closest companions carried their dying chief at his own request and secretly, towards Glastonbury, either in the hope of healing or to lay him in holy earth that held the bones of St Joseph of Arimathea and numerous saints. They carried him either along Arthur's Causeway, continuing by boat when the track dropped to the flooded plain; or, more probably, from the neighbourhood of Queen Camel to Ilchester (about four miles) and from there along eight miles of the Roman road past present-day Somerton to Street. A 9ft-wide Roman causeway constructed from stone, alder branches and oak piles (uncovered in the nineteenth century) ran parallel to the present road from Street to Glastonbury, set on its small eminence above the bog. A small bridge of oak spanned the Brue at the place now called Northover, somewhere near the spot where a very ordinary stone bridge—nowadays called Pomparles because one of the preceding bridges was most romantically named *Pons Perilis* in the fifteenth century—stands astride the insignificant trickle of the Brue. But in Arthur's day the Brue had not been embanked and spread its waters for much of the year in a wide lake across the

Pomparles: a view of the Bridge 1837; a vignette from Phelps's
Antiquities of Somersetshire

marshes, reaching back to the huge mere, five miles in circumference, that gave Meare its name.

Arthur, mortally wounded, made the superhuman effort of
staggering on to the bridge and flinging his great sword into the
lapping water. In the days before motorised traffic rushed over
Pomparles, one might see, on a night of marsh-mist and pallid
moonlight, a man with a cruel great gash on his brow stagger on
to the bridge and whirl his gleaming sword into the Brue.

After this last feat, Arthur—except in the opinion of those
who believed he was rowed, dying, over the shallow misted mere
towards a paradisal Avalon or Isle of Apples—was carried to the
little Celtic abbey where he died. With the knowledge only of
his closest fighting-companions and a few monks, he was laid in

74

a hollowed oak-trunk and reverently interred 16ft deep between two stone 'pyramids', or carved shafts of two crosses, in the cemetery on the south side of Joseph of Arimathea's wattle church. A burial so secret that 'men said Arthur was in another place and would come again'.

A few years afterwards, the corpse of the erring Guinevere— who had entered a convent and become an abbess—was carried by night in a sombre cortège from Amesbury to be laid close to Arthur. On dark nights the spectral flickering of the torches that lit the route for her bier have been seen moving along the road from Shepton Mallet above Glastonbury.

Six centuries later King Henry II, who had heard a Welsh bard sing of Arthur's end, ordered the abbot to dig for a hollowed oak-trunk between two carved stone pyramids south of St Joseph's Chapel. Monks set to work in an area screened-off by curtains. A long way down they turned up a stone slab, to which was fixed a small cross of Mendip lead with its engraved inscription facing inwards for concealment:

'Hic jacet sepultus inclitus Arturus Rex in insula Avallonia'.

Beneath it they found the hollow oak trunk, containing the bones of a man of gigantic stature; in its lower portion were the slender bones of a woman and a plait of shining golden hair that powdered to dust under a monk's exploring fingers. With the greatest reverence these poor remains of the great soldier-chieftain and his lovely, unfaithful wife were transferred to a black marble tomb, and housed in the Great Church of the Abbey.

A century later, in 1278, King Edward I came to Glastonbury on a ceremonial visit and to celebrate Easter, accompanied by his beloved queen, Eleanor of Castile. (When she died, the king raised seven sculptured 'Eleanor Crosses' resembling stone flowers along her funeral route to Westminster.) On the Tuesday of Easter week, King Edward ordered the sculptured double tomb at Glastonbury to be opened; and this was done as dusk enfolded cloisters and buildings. Two caskets were found inside, painted respectively with the arms and likeness of Arthur and Guinevere and containing their bones: Arthur's of great size, Guinevere's fine and slender. King Edward carried Arthur's bones and Queen Eleanor those of Guinevere, wrapped in silken cloths, in a solemn religious procession for the adoration of the awed crowd assembled in the abbey church. Then the silk-wrapped bones were reverently replaced in the caskets, which were sealed and again hidden in the marble tomb. This was set before the High Altar where it remained until ransacked by vandals after the Dissolution. In 1931, archaeologists re-discovered the cavity where the tomb once rested. This is visible today in the green turf enclosed by the abbey ruins and is clearly indicated.

The small leaden cross, only 1ft high, was set above the tomb, or on it, during the ceremony of 1278. It survived several centuries, even after the destruction of the tomb, as an object of curiosity and considerable veneration. The cross disappeared in Wells some time during the eighteenth century, its last owner was called Hughes; though perhaps this was only a replica. Miniature reproductions of it are still sold to tourists.

Arthur's name is in evidence in unexpected corners of Somerset. On the A371 road from Bruton to Shepton Mallet, near a signpost marked Castle Cary 2¾ miles, Ditcheat 1 mile, a little bridge bearing the name Arthur's Bridge stands where Arthur built one when he needed a ford. It is a very ordinary bridge of dark moss-stained stone, spanning the fast-flowing dark-green water of the river Alham that is edged with alders and ivy-wreathed firs.

Arthur's Oak grows in a lane at Edgarley, near Glastonbury. 'Nobody dare cut it down', said a boy who pointed it out. And some still believe that the tall figure of King Herod carved on the north doorway of St Mary's Chapel at Glastonbury Abbey represents Arthur; as Sir John Harington of Kelston, Queen

Elizabeth's godson, wrote: 'He [Arthur] was of stature very tall, as appears by the proportion of him left *as they say here in our countreye of Somerset,* in a door of a church by the famous Abbey of Glassenbury.'

ALFRED

During the winter of 877–8, in days of drenching rain and nights of muffling marsh-fog, King Alfred, aged twenty-seven, found himself a fugitive hidden in a strange corner of Somerset. He had few resources left except his own courage. The Danish invaders, ferocious as the dragons in whose likeness they carved the prows of their longships, had overrun his kingdom, putting settlements to fire and sword, demolishing churches and sacred images, terrorising peasants by riding like demons on their stolen horses to plunder crops and cattle, scattering Alfred's fighting-men and forcing many of his thanes into flight overseas.

Some forty years earlier the Norsemen had sailed up the Severn and landed in this same region on the river Parrett's right bank. The Saxons had put their women and cattle inside the fortified camp on top of tall Brent Knoll, and then defeated the Danes in a bloody fight near the foot of the hill at a place subsequently named Battleborough, where a farm preserves the name. It lies left of the A38 Bridgwater–Bristol road.

In 878 there seemed little hope that Alfred or his civilised institutions could prevail against such brutal odds. Exhausted by battle and defeat he had hidden on the isle of Athelney. Like Brent Knoll, Glastonbury Tor, the Polden Hills, and its own near neighbour, that cone-shaped green mount at the confluence of Tone and Parrett, now called Burrow Mump and crowned with a ruined church, the 'isle' was so called only because it rose above the encircling levels of the huge undrained morass of the central Somerset plain, extending from Mendips to Quantocks. The rivers Brue, Axe, Parrett, Tone and their feeding rivulets sheeted it with flood-waters all winter and in all wet seasons; the tidal Parrett added salt sea-water. Great reed-beds and osier-

77

beds, patches of coarse grass, mats of bog-plants and groves of willows were interspersed among streams and pools. Near the isle of Athelney lay a vast forest of alder, hazel, oak and sycamore, inhabited by deer and wild goats. Wild fowl and herons haunted the wet moors; pools and streams held eels, fish and otters. On these changed moors today place-names owe their origin to former flora and fauna and vanished natural features, for example, Eel Meadow, Frog Island, Greylake, Stathe (station for boats) and Aller (alder tree). The web of tracks over the swamps and their degree of safety were familiar only to local men; swineherds, osier-growers, fishermen, fowlers, makers of baskets and wicker eel-traps. Among these men the king lodged in a reed-thatched hovel, his identity known only to a few trusted thanes whose presence, with his own, gave Athelney its name, signifying 'Isle of Nobles'.

You may find it today by turning off the A38 at Huntworth and following a road alongside the sluggish Parrett, past a pumping-station and farmland drained by modern engineering, past fields where, in a rainy season, gulls and swans swim on the shining floods, down lanes bordered by ditches called rhines, and old pollard-willows shrouded in ivy. Modern drainage machinery is ruthlessly tearing up these willows which are a markedly characteristic feature of this landscape. Continue past orchards, over a bridge spanning the Tone, past withy-beds, past bundles of withies drying near cottage-walls, past redbrick chimneys of the boilers that buff them—that is, boil them until their own skins have dyed the inner rod brown—until you reach the parish of East Lyng. From a lay-by made from part of an old road thick with sedge, off the A361 from Lyng, you will see the long projecting knoll of Alfred's Athelney. It is marked by a memorial obelisk like a truncated stone, its inscription almost erased, that the lord of the manor, Sir John Slade, built near the farmhouse in 1801.

Here Alfred lay in comfortless seclusion during the winter and spring months of 877–8, while the victorious foraging Danes

camped with Guthrum, their leader, at Chippenham in Wiltshire. But one day, not long before Easter, Somerset people saw
twenty-three of the dreaded dragon-headed ships bringing yet
another force of Danish raiders to land at Combwich on the
Parrett estuary below the Quantock Hills, about twelve miles
west of Athelney. The muddy Combwich creek was dominated
by the fortified camp of Cynwit, marked Cynwit Castle on the
ordnance map. Situated four miles north-west of Bridgwater and
one mile from the south shore of the Parrett, this rough, humpy
piece of uncultivated, steeply rising ground is locally called Cannington Park, and attracts children every autumn with the heavy
blackberry harvest offered by its bramble-thickets that grow
thickly among fragments of drystone walling, the remains of the
old fortifications. Not many years ago people still referred to it
as 'the place where they came from Athelney to fight'. It can be
reached from Cannington village by the Hinkley Point road to
Combwich, or by a parallel road off the A39.

The raiders landed, led by their chieftain Hubba; the dragon-
ships lay in the Combwich creek or 'pill'. But the course of these
ships, with their unmistakeable carved prows had been observed
from the top of the Quantocks by Alfred's alderman Odda, leading Alfred's levies, six hundred strong, from West Somerset and
Devon. Odda's beacon-fire, on this or some later occasion, blazed
from Longstone Hill on the Quantocks above Holford village—
eight miles from Cannington on the A39. The remains of its for-
saken hearth lie under the bracken on the southern side of the
crest, but the 'long stone' lies inconspicuously near a group of
firs just past that well-known landmark, the line of wind-twisted,
riven Holford Beeches on this hilltop. Odda's camp gave the
name to Hodder's Combe, a lovely green valley where forget-
me-not, flowering rush and other moisture-loving flowers grow
by a stream crossed by stepping-stones and shaded by great
oaks; the adjacent oakwoods of Willoughby Cleeve belong to the
National Trust. Neighbouring Adder Wood also owes its name
to Odda. Combe and woods are reached by crossing the bowling

green or small common opposite the gates of Alfoxton Park.

Odda led his men towards Combwich, along the track of the Saxon warpath or 'herepath' snaking down from the hilltops above Over Stowey—part of the path is incorporated in the modern road called the Stowey Road, really an ancient name—towards Cynwit Castle. On ground below the camp, Odda met the Danes and was routed, so that he and his Saxon men were forced to flee without food inside the camp protected by stout earthworks. Hubba settled down to defeat them by siege, knowing that the camp had no water-supply and bidding his men guard the springs below.

Observing that half the raiding force had crossed to the other bank of the tidal Parrett and were unable to ford the river through the deep mud left at low tide, Odda was shrewd enough not to delay. 'The Christians rushed out like wild boars', said Asser, referring to the onslaught that Odda led downhill at dawn. Twelve hundred Danes were slaughtered, including Hubba himself, and the magic Raven war-banner woven by Hubba's three sisters was captured. Coats of mail and clothing were stripped from the corpses before the Saxon buried them. The place of burial became the modern quarry in the side of the smaller hill west of the hill-fort. Blasting operations left skeleton limbs gruesomely protruding from the grassy sides of a cup-shaped hollow; skeletal hands and legs became quite a familiar sight to blackberry-pickers. When blasting exposed whole skeletons, people thought they saw the signs of hacking with swords.

When Odda took his men back to the hills, a few scattered Danes united to bury Hubba as befitted a great chieftain, in a great circular barrow or tumulus piled with stones, raised near the shores of the Severn Sea in the vicinity of his death-place. It was given the Saxon name of Ubbalow or Ubbacoc, translatable as Hubba's Mound. Attempts have been made to identify several mounds as Ubbalow, including the old windmill-mound in a corner of a field on the left of the road from the village of Stockland to remote Stert on the coast. But the majority of people, whether scholars or not, always felt certain that Hubba's remains lay under the imposing round tumulus—called Wick Barrow by archaeologists and Pixies' Mound by everybody else— that swelled from the field named Pixy Piece.

For centuries this grave knew utter loneliness. Winds swaying its rough grasses blew off the grey sea at Stolford, where barefooted men pushed sledges, called mud-horses, over the glistening mud flats to fetch fish caught in nets hung on stakes. Near the mound was a rude stone barn, where men had seen pixy threshers in red caps, like the trolls, threshing corn with small flails by night, and the holy spring called Sidwells, dedicated to the virgin St Sidwell, martyred a century before Hubba's birth. Over many years labourers told their children the story of the ploughman, on his way to work one morning, who found a little brown-faced fellow perched on the mound, rocking himself over his diminutive 'peel', or baker's wooden shovel, and wailing, 'I've broken my peel'. At the sound of footsteps he vanished like a brown leaf in the wind, but the kind-hearted ploughman tied on the broken-off handle with a piece of string and left the mended peel on the mound, where next morning he found a little cake, smoking-hot from the oven, all ready for him.

In 1907, when archaeologists explored Pixies' Mound, local workmen were not over-anxious to be employed on the digging. After dark the music of pixy revellers had sometimes been heard coming from the mound. When digging revealed a circular wall 85 inches round, they felt sure they had found the pixies' house. Some of the diggers experienced bad luck or illness, as many local people had predicted, and were persuaded by wives not to return to the work. The enterprise was interrupted for a time; local inhabitants said King Edward VII himself had stopped it because it was so unlucky. People avoided the place when digging was resumed, but awed voices repeated tales of the 'finds' unearthed. 'A stone sword as long as a man's arm'; 'a wonderful bronze flagon'—these were quoted after the discovery of a flint knife and a beaker of red pottery decorated with a pattern made

F

by the impression of plaited grass.

The crouched skeleton finally removed from the interior—
and now housed with his beaker and dagger in the County
Museum at Taunton—was, for most people, Hubba the Dane
and for many remained so; since most barrows are found on a
height and this one was built close to the sea as a Viking would
wish. His resting-place was tidied up. Today, forlorn and hardly
visible under hawthorn and bramble, it can be found incongruously situated just inside the forbidden entrance-gates of
Hinkley Point nuclear station, close to the space where workers'
coaches wait. The trickling of St Sidwell's spring is faintly
audible. Over everything—spinneys and rookeries, Stolford
lanes, the grey and brown shingle-beaches, the modernised
ancient village of Combwich, where they used to build boats
thought to resemble those of the Norsemen—the giant reactors
preside.

Guthrum moved his Danes to the Polden Hills where he kept
an eagle eye on any movements from Alfred's marsh-girdled
fastness, since men would be bound to emerge at times to recon-
noitre and make raids for food. Alfred strengthened his little
stronghold by making defences at the place called simply Beorgh,
denoting the mount or Burrow Mump (sometimes called Barrow
Mount) which rises where the Tone joins the Parrett. Here he
made a bridge over the east end of the Parrett, hence the present
name Burrow (or Borough) Bridge. On the mump he built a
fort, almost certainly of wood, which was described as 'elevated,
serving as a watch-tower, elegant and of beautiful workmanship'
—nothing remains. An alternative Saxon name for this hill
meant 'lookout place', and if one climbs up to the ruins of the
part-medieval, part-eighteenth-century church one looks over a
huge expanse of Somerset. This fort and the entrenchments on
the hill protected a causeway running to slightly raised ground
at Othery, another island place in the marshes where Alfred
raised, not far from Athelney, a second and smaller protective
fort. The connecting causeway, which followed more or less the

course of the A361, was for most of the year covered by water. Only local people knew the passing-places. Alfred has even been credited with constructing the mump itself, which is often called Alfred's Fort, from stiff red soil found three miles away at Curry Rivel; as the mump's soil seems redder than that of surrounding land. Or, 'He built it with stuff from the rhines', old men used to say.

Gradually more Saxon fighting men found their way to Athelney, and Alfred led them on sorties to harass roving Danes. With more men, however, the food shortage became acute. Everyone knows the tale of the day when Alfred in his rough clothes sat by the cowherd's turf fire making some arrows, organising his campaign, and supposedly watching the flat cakes baking on the hearth, while the cowherd's wife gathered sticks. Arriving home to find the cakes unturned and blackened, she scolded him shrewishly until the cowherd appeared and quelled her, his look conveying more meaning than his words. In Wedmore church (B3151 from Street, B3139 from Wells) a stained glass window, commemorating Queen Victoria's Jubilee, depicts Alfred among other English monarchs; not only Alfred with sceptre and harp, Alfred with Guthrum the Dane, but Alfred burning the cakes on the cowherd's hearth. The King Alfred Inn at Burrow Bridge, with his crowned head painted in gold on its sign, has in its skittle alley an object which local men swear is the table on which the cakes were kneaded and at which they were eaten. It looks like a butcher's block made from a knotty piece of wych-elm trunk, and came from the ruins of a flooded cottage at Athelney. In the 1930s it was mentioned in an advertisement, 'Call and see the original King Alfred's table!' At that date a booklet was sold at the inn, illustrated by a picture of this object, labelled 'A Table 1000 years old'. Even today, *Alfred the Great,* a booklet on sale in Burrow Bridge church, alludes to 'a table at the inn'. One skittles team that plays in matches at the King Alfred Inn is named the Burnt Cakes Team.

Another, less popularly known story of the Athelney cowherd

Denewulf makes part of the Somerset canon of Alfred legends. He impressed the king so much by his native intelligence and by his resentment of his poor, cramped existence that, when Alfred's fortunes changed, Denewulf was placed in a seat of learning for several years; and, when he had become a considerable scholar, Alfred made him a bishop, though the monks of Winchester disdained to accept him as theirs.

There is a much later and prettified version of the 'cakes' story. At some unspecified time young King Alfred put on beggar's clothes, for a whim, and wandered alone in the district of North Newton, between North Petherton and Athelney, carrying only a cudgel for his protection. He encountered a sunburnt shepherd with a crook who took him for a sturdy vagrant and challenged him to fight; the 'beggar' was victor in the duel. The shepherd became friendly and told him what a kind master he had in the lord of Newton manor who gave his shepherds clouted cream from his red cows. There was work for the 'beggar' and fair wages, if he liked to accompany the shepherd to his cottage. Alfred accepted, went home with the shepherd and met his rosy-faced wife, Gillian, who set the new shepherd lad minding the cakes of bread baking on the hearth. When he let them burn she scolded him shrilly, boxed his ears and banished him to sleep in the loft over their outhouse. The king spent a wretched night lying on a pile of sheepskins under rafters hung with cobwebs. Fowls and geese shared his lodging and at dawn, when he had just fallen asleep, a crowing cock awoke him. The king drew out his hunting horn, that he had carried wrapped in a bundled-up cloak, blew it with all his might, so that its notes echoed far through the forest of alders and brought a hundred nobles galloping to the cottage door. The shepherd and Gillian came out in terror and fell on their knees to ask pardon. Alfred made a jest of the episode and gave the shepherd a hundred wethers. The grateful shepherd promised the king a milk-white lamb every year and from his wife's distaff enough spun wool to make the king a coat.

In spite of the victory at Cynwit, Alfred had to continue living in privation on his fortified isle, and there his mother Osburga came to join him for a time. They were alone on a day of freezing wintry weather, Alfred's men having gone on an expedition to watch for movements of pillaging Danes, when the appearance of a poor pilgrim with his staff startled them. How had he found his way over vast stretches of bog and flood, with no one to show him the causeways? When he begged for bread, Osburga, who feared he had come as a spy, told him to go on his way as they had only one loaf left. But Alfred intervened, telling her to give the beggar half the loaf and to put her trust in Christ who had worked the miracle of the loaves and fishes. The pilgrim departed, carrying his half-loaf. Alfred and his mother both fell asleep, for cold and privation had exhausted them. They dreamed an identical dream of a white-robed figure wearing a mitre who announced that he was Cuthbert, former Bishop of Lindisfarne, and bade the banished Alfred keep up his courage as he should be restored with honour to his throne. As a token of this, the fishermen of Athelney, who had set out with forlorn hopes that morning when the rivers and pools were locked in ice, would return with baskets full of fish. Osburga and her son awoke to find the fishermen already coming home with laden baskets, and knew that St Cuthbert had indeed appeared to them in Athelney.

Alfred had only to wait for his hour and to act when it came. When spring advanced he himself insisted on making 'scouting' expeditions among the Danes. He was young and must have felt a need to move from such narrow quarters, to know risk and action once again. He dressed in a woollen tunic and cloak, took his harp and set out as a wandering Saxon glee-man, whom even the Norsemen would spare if his music entertained them. He went at the time of neap tides when water was low in the marshes and entered their camp on the Poldens, and others farther afield, singing and playing to the fierce warriors, who rewarded him with mead and food while his ears and eyes absorbed information.

The noblest chiefs of Danish sway,
Charmed by his harp would pass the day,
And banish night to hear him play.

He returned unscathed to Athelney where, just before Whitsuntide, his scouts brought the joyful news that Wessex men of
three counties had responded to his summons by rallying at
Egbert's Stone, east of the great forest of Selwood, at Pen
Selwood in east Somerset. Moving from the west, the Wessex
men had set their signal beacons flaring at points along the
Quantock ridgeway: on Beacon Hill, on Longstone, and on the
hill called Crowcombe Fire Beacon, overlooking the Vale of
Taunton. From various districts men rallied to Alfred, converg-
ing one chilly night at Taunton, where they made great fires with
boughs chopped from the ash trees that grew so plentifully in
the Quantock area. They found that even when green the ash
would burn. Centuries later an annual winter ball, called the
Ashen Faggot Ball, was held at Taunton, during which a huge
ashen faggot was burned at midnight on the ballroom hearth.

Through a May night, Alfred with his little troop from
Athelney rode unhindered the thirty miles or so to Egbert's
Stone, that marked the junction of three shires. There they met
'the folk of Somerset, Wiltshire and Hampshire' who, feeling all
their hopes renewed as they waited among the old forest trees
green with new life, 'at sight of the king were filled with joy and
hailed him as one alive again from the dead'.

It would be useless to look for Egbert's Stone today, although
a boundary-stone stood on the site in 1804. It is said to have
been covered by a pond. However, in the eighteenth century, a
Hoare of Stourhead in Wiltshire built, near South Brewham,
the turreted brick tower, 155ft high, that is named Alfred's
Tower and stands near the meeting-place of the king's forces
where he raised his standard. An eighteenth-century statue of
Alfred looks down from a niche over its door.

Next day, in grey morning light, Alfred boldly led his West
Saxons out of Selwood towards the Polden Hills, where he would

fight his decisive battle against Guthrum and his pagans. The second night, Alfred camped about ten miles from his objective, at a place chronicled as Eglea or Iley. This was Eggarley, the present Edgarley, above Glastonbury on the A361. They lay near marshy ground and a wood of willows, with the Tor brooding above them; here in the night Alfred saw a ghostly vision of St Neot, whom he had known when the saint was alive and by whom he had been reproved for his sin of pride. This time the saint came to bring comfort and encouragement, telling the king that the Lord would fight for him and that St Neot himself would go the whole day ahead of Alfred's standard.

In morning mist, Alfred and his Saxons set out in silence to assault Guthrum and his much larger force massed at Ethandun, on what is now Edington Hill above the Sedgemoor fenland; the parish of Edington is partly on the moor, partly on the Polden Hills. Over the hill—in wedge formation, making a great wall of shields, with spears flashing in early morning sunlight the Saxons launched a fierce attack in the rear of the surprised Danes. Alfred, it is said, fought as if he were more than mortal, yet at one time the issue seemed doubtful. At a crucial moment St Neot appeared, seized the dragon-standard and fought by Alfred's side. After immense slaughter, the Danish survivors fled, hotly pursued, in a north-westerly direction along the ridgeway that ended at a steep bluff and a walled camp, called Downend or Chisley Mount (both names are still used by archaeologists). Guthrum shut himself and as many of his men as possible within the camp's earthworks and moat; it was a strongly fortified place, used by Britons and Romans, and had a spring so that they could hold out for a while. But they had no food; Alfred held the ridgeway, and not one of the Danes unlucky enough to be shut outside the gates was left alive. The camp was near the place now called Dunball, where the making of the railway erased many ancient features, while Sir John Moulton, in 1677, arbitrarily cut the loop of the river Parrett, that made a creek, where ships anchored below the camp. Guthrum's ships were lying in this creek, later named Viking's Pill; the flocks and oxen he had captured pastured on a grassy isle in the marshes that well-nigh surrounded it, but these availed him nothing. After a fortnight's siege the Danes surrendered, offering many hostages and not daring to demand any.

A twelfth-century Norman poet knew of the Battle of Ethandun, now called Edington:

> E lendemain, à hure de none,
> Donc sont venuz à Edenesdone.

As at Combwich, old men at Edington used to remark: 'They of Athelney fought here.'

Beside the A39, running along the Polden ridge towards Glastonbury, Chilton Polden Priory—misnamed and unmistakeable because it was built as a folly—stands opposite the Edington battle-site. If you follow the road branching off opposite the Priory, signposted to Sutton Mallet and Stawell, a little distance downward, you will reach a crossroads where one lane is marked Billicombe Lane. On the right, a piece of slightly rising ground beyond a hedge of maple is called Righton's Grave and is marked on the map; there is no sign of a mound, but here, below Cock Hill, Alfred buried the slaughtered Danes.

Railway navvies working near the camp at Downend shovelled out bones 'by the bushel' in their own estimation. The old fortress is reached by turning off the Bridgwater–Pawlett stretch of the A38 at its junction with the road to Puriton village.

Alfred's peace terms included Christian baptism for pagan Guthrum and his Viking chieftains. Accordingly, seven weeks later, Guthrum and thirty Danes came to the place called Aller, in the marshes between the Tone and Parret, with woods of alders growing round it. Not far from the little town of Langport, Aller still has the quality of remoteness. If you go down its long street of stone cottages—one with a fine straw pheasant on its thatched roof—you will see no sign of the church, unless you turn off by the inn with the big tree outside and take a fairly long walk towards the farms. The church, cheek-by-jowl with a farm, is the place, if not the building, where the wild Norsemen received 'the laver of baptism'. The Saxon font, claimed to be the one actually used, was restored to the church in 1862, after the newly appointed rector had noticed a huge, primitive-looking bowl, made from a block of Ham stone, with weeds growing inside and ivy smothering it, lying on its side among a clutter of stones in the rectory garden. It was undamaged except for a break in its lip. Very curiously, a rounded plinth with a pierced shaft was discovered later in a dark corner of the belfry and fitted the bowl perfectly. The font stands near the Norman door.

Close to this sacred receptacle the Danish jarls knelt, until Alfred raised up Guthrum who was now his godson and given the name Athelstan. Afterwards Alfred entertained the baptised Danes as honoured friends at his royal villa at Wedmore, at that time another fenland island surrounded by water for much of the year, now a large and very handsome village. Here, in accordance with the rites of baptism, the chrism or holy oil was poured on the converts' heads, and white fillets, the chrism-cloths, bound round their brows to protect the oil for seven days. Then came the ceremony of 'chrism-loosing' when the white bands were removed. Four more days' rejoicing, then the Danes departed with generous gifts that included work by Alfred's goldsmiths.

Those who seek the place where Alfred had his summer palace as it is always called, find themselves directed to unromantically-named Mudgley, on the slope of a hill between Theale and Badgworth, on the B3139 from Wells. It is a diminutive hamlet in Wedmore parish, 1½ miles from Wedmore church. A local tradition that Alfred's bones were carried to Wedmore for burial—in a gold coffin—stems from their removal from Winchester to Hyde Abbey and their dispersal by vandals of a later age. While the writer was standing near a field-gate in a lane at Mudgley, where another lane overgrown with briars bears the Saxon-flavoured name White Horse Lane, a courteous old man cutting

The road into Alfred's Palace, Mudgley, Wedmore; a drawing from
The Wedmore Chronicle 1887

a hedge asked if she was trying to find 'the place where King Alfred is buried' and gave her directions.

No, Mudgley is not Alfred's burial-place, yet many believe his palace stood in the sloping field overlooking the turf-moors. The site still commands a great sweep of green plain, drained now and dotted with brown-tiled stone farms, orchards, groups of trees and spiked with pylons. The field, where hooves of grazing cattle soon churn the soil to peat-black mud, has the lovely name of Court Garden and is joined on the south by another, called King's Close. Until 1818, when the road to Glastonbury cut through, it joined Court Garden Orchard across the road and another field patterned with lines of reeds and smaller ditches, known as grypes. Court Garden is bounded by a stream and large, rude

The underground chamber, Mudgley, Wedmore; a drawing from
The Wedmore Chronicle 1887

stones strew the grassy ground.

Alfred's palace extended right across to Court Garden Orchard and whatever is left of it lies underground, unless the strewn
stones came from its walls. A hundred years ago investigators
found three thick walls of an underground room measuring 20ft
by 16ft standing in a walled courtyard with a well. They found
a hearth, pigs' bones, mussel-shells; arrow-heads and a spur; four
keys, two of them near their doors. Alfred's? They found no
gold coffin, as some people had expected. But they unearthed
an old road made of stones, hidden by soil, that led over the field
to the courtyard. The hedge-cutter who mentioned Alfred said
that one can see parts of this rough-paved track now when the
ground is not too muddy.

In pious gratitude for his victory, King Alfred built a small monastery at Athelney, on the low ridge where Denewulf's hut had stood, and where today there is a farmhouse. He made his mass-priest, John, its first abbot. Its church was of unusual design, with four supporting piers and four circular chancels. We are told that Athelney monks were 'few, indigent and delighted in solitude', a true description, no doubt, of men who consented to come to a place 'with only two acres of dry land'. The first monks were foreigners, as no native inhabitants had piety enough to submit to living there. Athelney is in the parish of East Lyng, where in the church belfry the tomb-slab of an Athelney monk called Benedict used to lie.

Not a stone remains of Alfred's abbey or of its successors—even the isle itself has shrunk since Alfred's day—but a memorial to it exists among the rhines and reeds near the layby off the A361, mentioned earlier. Inside a muddy drove a rough block of blue lias displays a metal plaque inscribed:

> The Hill behind this Plaque
> is believed to be the Site
> of the Abbey built by
> King Alfred as a Thanksgiving
> For the Defeat of the Danes
> in AD 878

The last remnant of Athelney Abbey was Adscombe Chapel, in Over Stowey parish in the Quantocks, which belonged to the abbey and housed half-a-dozen brothers. For centuries its ivy-mantled ruins stood in a field not far from Seven Wells Combe, and the last grey wall was demolished only a few years back. A ghostly monk used to be seen in the combe at twilight.

Countless stories have been told about objects dug or ploughed up on the abbey site: pieces of freestone carved, painted, gilded; a yellow tile patterned with a white lily; a small corroded copper figure of Christ; a stone coffin and a skull; daggers and spurs. Eighteenth-century labourers, employed on removing the ruins, suddenly prospered; according to their neighbours, they had found a gold spur, which they 'disposed of to their own advantage' and which was never seen again. There were stories too of a golden spear, 'the gift of Alfred' that likewise vanished.

One exquisite object, a masterpiece of Saxon art, did turn up in 1693 in a field, called Parkersfield, in the parish of North Newton four miles north-west of Athelney. The Alfred Jewel, as it is known, was described as 'this ancient picture of St Cuthbert made by order of King Alfred' when Oxford University received it from Mr Palmer, of Fairfield House, Stogursey. It is now in the Ashmolean Museum, but the churches of East Lyng and North Petherton possess replicas. It consists of an oval rock crystal set in a frame of exquisitely-worked gold. Under the crystal there is a half-length figure, crowned and enthroned, in semi-transparent enamels, green, red and yellow; in each hand the figure holds either a fleur-de-lis or a sceptre surmounted by a flower. The legend round the border reads

AELFRED MEC HEHT GEWIRCAN
(Alfred had me made)

Numerous explanations have been put forward as to its uses and how it came to lie under the soil of a field near Athelney for eight centuries. Some say that the Jewel adorned Alfred's helmet and that he lost it in a fight with a band of Danes. Some say that he wore it in his crown, as illustrated by stained glass in a window of Lyng church; that he brought the Jewel to Athelney to prove his kingship, and that he, or a messenger, threw it away or hid it when in danger of being captured. Others contend that Alfred wore it round his neck on a cord as an amulet. But the majority believe that it was the elaborate handle of an 'aestel' or horn pointer used for following passages in a book, like Alfred's English version of *Cura Pastoralis*, (*The Herdsman's Book*) of which he gave a copy, with a costly pointer, to every bishop in his kingdom.

Yet the Jewel was made at Alfred's special command by an

outstanding Saxon master of the goldsmith's craft and, as the figure enshrined in the crystal is that of St Cuthbert who came to Athelney in beggar's guise, the legend most commonly believed is that Alfred gave the Jewel to his priest, John, the Abbot of Athelney and that a monk trying to save this treasure from Henry VIII's spoilers fled across the marshes to hide it.

St Cuthbert is a rare figure in the iconography of Somerset churches. His head is next to Dunstan's in a tracery light of the south-east window of the Ladychapel in Wells Cathedral. He is paired again with Dunstan in sepia-coloured medieval glass at Cothelstone church, a few miles from Taunton. Here three windows present six English saints, two in the top lights of each window, and Cuthbert is seen in a window of the Stawell chapel, holding a crozier in one hand and, in the other, the crowned head of St Oswald, King of Northumbria.

Alfred, lover of books and deeply religious, carried his *Manual of Devotions* even in the Somerset marshes. He is depicted carrying it in the stained glass of two or three Somerset church-windows.

Somerset did not enjoy complete freedom from the Danish terror until AD 1000; during their series of invasions, grim little legends were scattered along the coast and in the Quantock area like a raven shedding his black feathers. The Danes had a piratical lair on barren Steep Holm in the Severn Sea, and sailed over to Bleadon and Uphill, where they tied up their ships in the creeks and marched inland to plunder provisions while the inhabitants hid in fear. Uphill is supposed to have been named Hubba's Pill because of its associations with the Danish chieftain. Desperate with hunger, a lame old woman of Bleadon emerged from a hole in the rocks, crept with her knife from ship to ship, cutting their cables so that they drifted out to sea with the tide. The Danes were massacred while trying to reach them. Over the years, their teeth and skulls have been turned up from the soil by ploughmen.

The prow of each Danish ship was carved in a dragon's likeness, which formed the root of the centuries-old Dragon of Aller story still current in this frequently ravaged area. This poison-breathing monster, which had the shape of a great flying serpent and was protected by an armour of scales, lived in a den in the south side of Round Hill above Aller. It descended to devastate the villages in the marshy valley, and wherever it flew the crops and trees were poisoned. Milkmaids fled at the first hiss of its wing-beat; a score of pails had their contents drunk in a few minutes. People lived in dread of a horrible death for themselves, their children and their cattle. At last a knight called John of Aller, or the Lord of Aller, came boldly to their rescue. He plastered his body with pitch and put on a mask so that the dragon's breath could not harm him; he armed himself with a long spear specially fashioned for his exploit, journeyed to the dragon's den and attacked the monster while it slept. After a fierce fight in the darkness, he killed it. Seeing two or three baby-dragons in the den, he went home to fetch several of his labourers to help him stop up the hole with the spikes of an iron harrow. After that day nothing would grow near the hollow place in the hill except elder-trees, the 'elderns' that are considered sinister and sometimes connected with Danes. Some who relate the legend declare that 'the Aller Dragon was slain by a harrow'.

In the north wall of the chancel of Aller church a modern one-light window commemorates Alfred, who is wearing a blue cloak and standing with his sword held as if it were a cross. The glass over his head displays a letter A. Below this window there is an upright slab beautifully incised with bold lettering and heraldry; near by, in a cusped recess, there lies a defaced effigy of a knight, with his dagger suspended by two cords from a richly ornamented baldrick. He, they say, is John of Aller who killed the dragon; and the spear he used, by an astonishing chance, still exists. At one time it was kept in the belfry of Aller church, but to see it now you must continue on the A372 to a place called Wearne, about a mile before reaching Langport; take the turning to Low Ham and walk to the church set in the middle of the fields, with cattle grazing outside its doors. Ralph Stawell, Baron of Somerton, rebuilt this church in the seventeenth century; inside, behind the iron railing round his tomb, leans the spear that slew the Aller Dragon. It is a kind of dart 9ft long, made of light wood, its shaft curiously painted in a band-pattern of brown, green and yellow with rings of black between.

It is rather curious that Herb Robert, the pretty, rosy plant of the hedge-banks, used to be called Dragon's Blood in parts of Somerset near North Petherton.

Gruesome tales are related about the flaying of Danes, who, if caught robbing Christian churches, had their skins nailed on the doors as a horrible warning—like that given to thievish birds by the gamekeeper's nailed-up bodies of jay and magpie. The former private museum at Chilton Polden Priory (or Folly) possessed the old iron-clad door of Stogursey church which had a Dane's skin nailed upon it. In the beautiful church at Mark, neighbour to Wedmore on the B3139 from Wells to Highbridge, as late as the 1930s, there was a chest with a covering of hide rubbed very thin, said to be a portion of a Dane's skin nailed on the church door over a thousand years earlier, after his execution for stealing the silver chalice.

Several battle-stories hang round a field, Walford Down, just outside Curry Rivel, where red elders used to grow abundantly. Red elder, the popular name of Dwarf Elder, or *Sambucus Ebulus*, is so called because its leaves turn fiery crimson in the autumn. Its Somerset names are Danewort, Daneweed and Danes' Blood. The most persistent legend holds that a battle took place there and that the luxuriant growth of red elders sprang from the blood of slaughtered Danes. 'They red elders have growed about there ever since' is an old woman's remark quoted early in the present century. Others assert that red elders grow rankly on the graves of Danes, from which they derive an evil smell and noxious properties. John Aubrey said they grew abundantly near Chippenham where Danes were slain in a battle with Alfred.

The red elders at Curry Rivel are, however, mentioned in a story of a milkmaid who, in the time of the Civil War, went out

Page 97 (*above*) Fragment of St Aldhelm's Cross, Bath;
(*below*) Solsbury Camp or Little Solsbury, near Bath

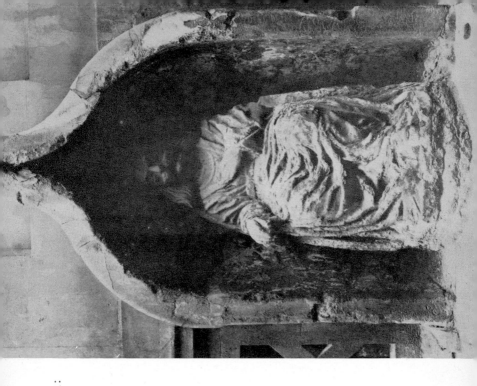

Page 98
(*left*) St Dunstan:
gilded wooden
figure from the
barge of The
Worshipful
Company of
Goldsmiths;
(*right*) statue of
Bladud, Bath

early one summer morning to milk her cows in the field. She ran shrieking home because her feet were dabbled not with dew but with blood on account of the previous night's battle.

Dane's Combe, alternatively called Smith's Combe, is named as another scene of an affray with Danes; it runs off the A39 Bridgwater–Minehead road opposite the lane to East Quantoxhead, and lies below Beacon Hill. Danesborough, alternatively called Dowsborough, is the highest but one of the Quantock Hills and the site of an Iron Age camp, a wonderful lookout post over the sea. It stands above little Dodington on the A39 and is reached via the old Coach Road, branching off not far from the Castle of Comfort, formerly an inn, between Nether Stowey and Holford. A beautiful, continually climbing walk brings you to its slopes, brown with scrub-oak; there, it is said, Danish marauders who had come inland from Combwich were wiped out. Their ghosts live on in the hill's interior below the camp on the summit; whortleberry-pickers and furze-cutters going home late sometimes heard their wassail songs and wild laughter issuing from the heart of the hill, while others heard the blowing of horns sounded as if in battle.

At one time the conquering Danes were lured by women of this neighbourhood to their homes as lovers, and murdered during the night. But one girl fell in love with a flaxen-headed Danish boy, who had fled before the battle with his harp slung on his shoulder, and sheltered him for several days until he was discovered and killed. It was said afterwards that his ghost roamed the sunset slopes of Danesborough, faintly singing or plucking the strings of his harp, and that at times a startled hill pony pricks his ears at soft movements in the bracken and the notes of a muted song. Wordsworth, who often walked near Danesborough, seems to have heard about the phantom Danish boy, wearing a fur vest 'in colour like a raven's wing'—significant detail—with the harp slung from his shoulder, who, as he wanders the hillside,

> ... warbles songs of war
> That seem like songs of love.

G

A persistently credited legend, however, exists that a number of Danes settled among villagers along the coast from Lilstock to Watchet, which remained extremely isolated until the coming of twentieth-century transport. Even the place-names—Wick, Lilstock, Stert, Stolford—are believed to smack of the invaders. Whether the Norsemen lingered, or stayed only a single night, they are said to have fathered children whose descendants have red hair, so that the epithet 'Dane's bastard' was flung at a redheaded person as a term of insult.

This association with resident Norsemen created a number of local legends. At the Parrett end of the 'herepath' running from the Quantocks to Combwich, in the shadow of Cynwit Castle, the field-paths were long avoided after dark when the 'wild hunt' might be encountered; the traveller would cower back and cover his face until the headless rider on his black horse, and his demon pack of black hounds with tongues of red flame, had swept by. They were seen even in the thick mist of an autumn dawn by a shepherd, mistakenly opening a gate for a rider. People in lonely cottages heard the baying of hounds on a windy night. A man passed a headless rider on a silent black horse under the trees of a lane and learned next day that the old Combwich 'witch-woman' had died; he had seen the Devil 'coming to fetch her'. The Devil riding a sow was another fearful apparition encountered near the camp, although misfortune could be avoided by pronouncing the Holy Name. To brush past the silent black ghost-dog, who sometimes roamed at night, brought the worst luck of all.

These stories are believed to have been brought by the Norsemen from their native land. They also gave the name Wayland's Pool to the peaty-brown, branch-overhung pool, often sought by deer, in Shervage wood (now National Trust property, on the A39 near Holford). On a still night, the faint hammering of a ghostly anvil has been heard somewhere in the recesses of this lovely wood of oaks and beeches that is the setting of a long-established dragon-legend. A fearful dragon living there terrorised the farms and villages, until a woodman, sitting down on what he thought was a rough and knotted tree trunk, found himself astride the scaly monster and valiantly killed it with his axe as it started to breathe fire.

The pretty little cottage on the corner of the lane to Fiddington, off the A39 between Cannington and Nether Stowey, was the Keenthorne smithy, well within living memory. All the local people knew the ancient legend of a cloaked traveller one dark night demanding that the smith shoe his horse and promising silver. The smith started work but, seeing a cloven hoof beneath the man's cloak, ran away in terror, on the pretext of fetching a hammer. He was saved by the village priest, who told him to take no payment and stood close by him to combat the devil's power.

One night, during one of their last incursions, the Danes raided and burnt Watchet, then streamed in an exultant horde along the coast to a place not far from Doniford cliffs, now inside the parish of Williton (ten miles from Minehead on the A39). They plundered and burned as they went, but Saxon soldiers emerged from fortified positions and killed all those unable to reach the coast and swim to their ships. The field of this bloody conflict is called Battlegore to this day. North of Williton the road divides, both routes leading to Watchet; the field lies beside the lefthand fork road opposite the large building of Williton School. It is rough land, almost like common, backed by a dark band of woodland. Not far from its gate a lichened stone bridge spans a fast, sullen-coloured stream. The large round mound surrounded by traces of earthworks near the centre of the field has long been called the burial place of the Danes who fought there, and has yielded up some bones.

On its south side, at a distance, three large slabs of red sand-stone—one measures 10ft—lie prostrate near the hedge. One stone stood upright in the nineteenth century when three big round mounds were still visible. Long before Dane or Saxon set foot on Battlegore, these stones were hurled by the Devil and a giant when 'having a match' as they stood on the Quantock Hills;

one still bears the print of the Devil's hand.

There must be as many devil-legends in Somerset as there are legends of saints; one of these concerns Baron Stawell, whose tomb is in Low Ham church. Monstrously extravagant, he had sold manor after manor, in most reckless fashion, so as to rebuild his father's mansion near Low Ham church, but on such a grandiose scale that after his death his trustees were obliged to let the unfinished house fall into ruin. Some of the walls in Low Ham fields are made from its stones. During Lord Stawell's lifetime an old fiddler lived in Low Ham who was in great demand to play at rustic weddings and celebrations. One Christmas Eve, after playing at a village dance until midnight, he was trudging home through cold, leafless lanes when a carriage and pair came driving at breakneck speed down the lane. The coachman pulled up his foaming horses as they approached the fiddler, who had shrunk close to the hedge. A richly-dressed gentleman thrust his peruked head out of the carriage window and asked him courteously enough if he was the renowned fiddler from Low Ham. When he faltered 'Yes, sir', the gentleman asked him persuasively if he would play at a ball that he was giving at his house on Christmas night. A carriage would fetch him from the lane and drive him home after the ball; he would be paid a handsome fee. The fiddler, less frightened now and very flattered, consented.

On Christmas night the coachman drove him miles along dark lanes and winding byways till they reached a mansion blazing with lights and ringing with the laughter of gaily-dressed revellers. The fiddler played for their dancing until well into the small hours, when they crowded round him, praised his playing and collected a bagful of gold for him. Before the delighted fiddler went out to the waiting carriage, the smiling host told him that he must see the treasures of his great house. He courteously conducted him through many rooms, all well-lit and adorned with rich carpets and priceless furniture. When they entered a luxurious bedroom that held a great bedstead of gold, the fiddler noticed a strange and sinister smell of burning. When he touched the bedstead, it burned his hand. There seemed to be a fire kindled beneath it. As he stared in terror, the gentleman said to him: 'This bed awaits Lord Stawell whose sins are many.'

He took the trembling fiddler to the carriage and drove the horses himself, at the speed of wind. 'Do not speak of what you saw,' he commanded. As he alighted, the fiddler noticed with horror that the gentleman had cloven hooves.

All night he tossed sleepless, thinking fearfully of the Devil's revenge if he ignored his warning. At daybreak he decided, in spite of his fears, to warn the debauched Lord Stawell that he was in peril of hell-fire. He showed him the bag of gold coins that he had received as a fee for his music. Lord Stawell listened, heeded and began to reform his way of life, building almshouses for the poor and rewarding the courageous fiddler, who threw away the devil's gold.

Almost a fairy story, but it is more recent than most.

3

'King' Monmouth and
the Western Rising

James Scott, Duke of Monmouth, was the oldest illegitimate son, and a great favourite, of Charles II. Handsome, vain, dissolute, he was a born intriguer, and soon after the accession of his uncle, James II, claimed the throne on the grounds that his mother had been Charles's lawful wife. Claiming also to be champion of the Protestant faith, he won widespread support in the west country where the numerous Dissenters had suffered persecution. During triumphal progresses in the west, he was lavishly entertained by several prominent families who, however, gave him little assistance during the rebellion. Many Taunton inhabitants, especially the Puritan weavers, rallied to his cause with enthusiasm, as did men from Bridgwater, Wellington, Glastonbury and other towns, while hundreds of misguided farm-workers and craftsmen from Dorset and Somerset rose to fight for him with improvised weapons, no training, and indifferent leadership.

Before the rising, he was proclaimed king in Taunton with great rejoicing, and received several deputations that included a procession of little girls. Dressed in white and bearing banners embroidered with a gold crown and the initials JR for Jacobus Rex, these girls were pupils at an academy kept by Mrs Susanna Musgrave and Miss Sarah Blake, sister of the great admiral. Miss Blake led them, and presented a Bible and a sword to the duke. At one time the Somerset County Museum possessed a miniature of Elizabeth Broadmead, of Wilton near Taunton, who had walked in the procession and was said to be one hundred and fifteen years old when she was painted.

In July 1685 the duke and his forces retreated from Bristol to Bridgwater. The story goes that William Sparkes, a Sedgemoor farmer, climbed onto the church tower at Chedzoy and surveyed the surrounding landscape with a 'spy-glass' which is now in the Blake Museum, Bridgwater. He saw the royal forces encamped on Sedgemoor near Weston Zoyland, four miles south-east of Bridgwater, and sent a slow-witted countryman called Richard Godfrey to inform Monmouth, who verified the news by looking out through a telescope from the roof of the lofty tower of St Mary's church. He decided to attack that night, 5 July. Unluckily for Monmouth, Godfrey had failed to mention the Bussex Rhine or ditch that defended the royalist army. Set in that region of lushly green Somerset lowlands called Sedgemoor, Weston Zoyland today is hardly recognisable as the small remote village to which the Duke of Monmouth and his followers came in 1685. Yet until the Second World War, when an airfield was built outside the village—its runway remains—it had not greatly changed. Housing estates have since filled its spaces and spread around it, so that it serves as a 'dormitory' for the now industrialised old market-town of Bridgwater. The soaring splendid church-tower still dominates the village and the broad surrounding plain, and even now there are times when the atmosphere of remoteness is still perceptible.

On 6 July, in the stillness and sunlight of evening, if you are approaching Weston Zoyland on the A372 from Bridgwater, you may catch the sound of hymn-singing—O God our help in ages

105

past, or some other hymn equally familiar to Anglicans and non-conformists at remembrance ceremonies—floating towards the main road from a place several hundred yards away on your left. The last lefthand turn on the outskirts of the village will take you directly towards Sedgemoor—drained, enclosed and reclaimed as rich farmland since the time of the battle—by way of a rutted trackway called Penzoy Drove, between fields of grazing cattle bounded by 'rhines' or ditches full of aquatic plants and bordered by scores of pollard willows. In the small hours of that July morning in 1685, some of the rebels must have stumbled down this drove, seeking escape through marsh mist whitened by moonlight. At the end, another track with the primitive-sounding name of Zog Drove branches right, and a short distance along it another, called Langmoor Drove, turns left to the battlefield.

The Bussex Rhine, the broad dyke so fatal to Monmouth's enterprise, is now only a long, wide, slightly hollow, dry course, in which water lies only after wet weather, running across land on the right of Zog Drove. A gipsy-woman encountered in a Somerset lane during Monmouth's triumphal 'progress' in 1680 had warned him 'Beware of the rhine'. He had thought she meant the river Rhine. Had she been a Somerset woman, she would have pronounced it 'reen'.

A great circular grave mound, covered with sand from a pit on Bussex Farm, was revealed in 1850 after the earth subsided below the moorland surface; this gave rise to some grim stories of living wounded being flung in with the dead, all stripped naked. This vanished mass grave lay not far away from the place where on 6 July a small crowd of people from several villages gathers in front of the Sedgemoor memorial stone, with a choir, children carrying banners, the Vicar of Weston Zoyland and a nonconformist minister, to celebrate a simple service of remembrance, rounded off by the sounding of the Last Post and Reveille. Most members of this assembly will be familiar with the legends and traditions concerning that ill-starred affair called the Monmouth Rebellion. For inhabitants of the Sedgemoor country, even in modern times, the stories are part of their regional inheritance.

This open-air congregation stands on ground that is the core of a large mass of traditional narrative concerning participants in the Western Rising. In 1927 Mr Oliver Reed, of Weston Zoyland, gave a plot of the 'Graveyard Field', or 'Graveyards' as it was sometimes called, as a site for a memorial, a flagstaff was erected, and two limes planted that now sway and whisper over the heads of the congregation. In 1928 the Stone of Memory, a rough slab of Cornish granite, was raised near the lime trees; and in 1929 four staddles of Ham stone, that had previously supported stacks of unthreshed wheat, were brought from Yeabridge Farm, South Petherton, and placed as corner-pinnacles. Rather incongruously these staddles were inscribed with names of battles, such as Plassey, that took place later than the Monmouth Rebellion. The granite memorial stone bears the inscription:

> To the Glory of God
> And in Memory of All Those Who
> Doing the Right as they Gave it [sic]
> Fell in the Battle of Sedgemoor
> 6th July 1685
> And Lie Buried in this Field
> or Who for their Share in the Fight
> Suffered Death
> Punishment or Transportation
> Pro Patria

Miss Elizabeth Winter, of Chedzoy, organised the public subscription that paid for the monument and, as if everything connected with the rebellion needs to be invested with legend, the story is told that inspiration came to her as she lay weeping in the middle of the night because her collie dog had been injured and destroyed. A voice spoke to her: 'You weep for your dog. What of my poor lambs lying unmourned and unremembered in your fields?'

She set about raising a memorial fund.

In the confusion, noise and despair of the battle, Monmouth put off his armour and rode for dear life through the wreathing marsh-mist, side by side with his officer Lord Grey, and followed by his physician, Dr William Oliver, a German count and his brave servant, William Williams. Their horses' hooves beat softly on the moist black soil of the moors as they galloped towards the little village of Chedzoy, leaping the gleaming dykes, swerving to avoid trees in the mist, riding over small Brentsfield Bridge where Monmouth's horse began to flag. The duke was supplied with money from Williams's store, but his cloak 'with ye starr on'—probably the Garter—had been left on the battle-field. Before Monmouth took it off, he had ridden along a line of men. A bayonet caught and tore off a piece of his cloak to which was sewn one of its globular buttons covered with gold thread. Two of his men divided this relic after the battle; one cherishing the rag of cloth, the other the button, as souvenirs of their lost leader. In old age the owner of the button said that he wanted it placed in his coffin but finally gave it to his vicar at Congresbury. It can be seen, with its gold thread tarnished, in the Blake Museum, Bridgwater.

The fugitives knocked at a sleeping farmhouse, unidentifiable today although its owner is known to have been an ancestor of rich William Stradling, builder of Chilton Polden Priory, where numerous Monmouth relics were housed in his private museum. A fresh horse was requested and supplied. While saddle and bridle were put on, the duke stepped into the house and removed his collar with the decoration of the order of St George given him by his royal father, hiding the 'George' in his clothing. After his capture, Sir William Portman found it there; it helped establish the fugitive's identity. The sound of voices awoke a two-year-old boy who stared at the tall haggard man standing in the candlelight. The duke had a blue ribbon fastened with a silver buckle round his neck. It was a lover's keepsake, the girdle of his mistress Henrietta Wentworth, who had embroidered it herself. Now he hung it round the child's neck, picked him up and kissed him. 'This may be of use to you some day,' he said. 'Or I can have it again.'

For many years afterwards Somerset countrypeople, unshaken in their belief in Monmouth's kingship, came to touch the silver buckle to be cured of the malady called the king's evil. The same faith had impelled Elizabeth Parcet, the twenty-year-old daughter of a poor Crewkerne widow, to walk to Hinton St George, a very beautiful village in south Somerset, one day in that radiant summer of 1680 when the duke made his progress through Somerset and was enthusiastically entertained. Elizabeth Parcet had suffered from the evil for ten years, and had six running wounds in one arm and hand, as well as one eye badly affected, so that she could not work to help support the other children in the family or to earn money for a visit to London for King James to touch her. Hearing of Monmouth's visit she declared: 'But certainly I should be well if I could but touch him.' Her mother let her go although surgeons' aid had proved useless and so had the alleged healing powers of a man who was a seventh son.

At Hinton, Sir John Sydenham feasted the duke and a crowd of friends under the trees of the park of Hinton House, the seat of his young Poulett nephew. As Monmouth and his happy entourage left the park, surrounded by a throng of applauding country folk all wearing sprays of green leaves in his honour, Elizabeth Parcet pushed her way through the staring people, pulling off the glove that covered her diseased hand so that her bare hand could clutch Monmouth's wrist that also happened to be ungloved. 'God bless your greatness.'

'God bless you, my girl,' he replied, with the good-humoured grace of his Stuart father.

Her wounds dried up miraculously, leaving scars as evidence. Her eye became healthy. Neighbours and the Crewkerne minister all certified the miracle and thus strengthened Monmouth's claim to royalty.

His silver buckle is also in the Blake Museum, Bridgwater, in a carved case with the button. Hinton church contains several

striking and ornate tombs of the Poulett family who lived at
Hinton House until a few years ago. Hinton St George is reached
by an unclassified road off the A356 that runs through Crewkerne.

Dawn streaked the sky when the fugitives rode out on to the
Bath road, over Crandon Bridge and up on to the Polden ridge,
where Monmouth looked down on the green vista of Sedgemoor
and as the mist rolled away saw the last smoke of the battle in
which some of his deserted followers still struggled. For some
reason he and his companions turned southward towards the
village of Greinton. This is on the A361 and reached by the
side-road marked 'Greinton' near Loxley Woods on the right-
hand side of the Polden ridgeway as one travels from Bridgwater
on the Bath road, A39. Greinton is a village with a long street
and several handsome farmhouses set under the Polden ridge on
Sedgemoor's rim, yet no one knows the site of Greinton Gate
Farm owned by Thomas Bryant who received the fleeing Monmouth. It was sketched in ruins in 1772. Here Monmouth
obtained rest and refreshment, or other help, and left behind a
snuffbox inlaid with tortoise-shell and of Spanish workmanship.
Miss Eileen Bishop, a Bryant descendant, gave this to the
County Museum and it can now be seen in the Bridgwater
Museum. Nor does anyone know where the poor Greinton shepherd's one-storey hut called Edge House stood; this too was
depicted in a ruined condition in 1772. Here, some claim, supported by an illustration in an eighteenth-century magazine,
Monmouth put on the shepherd's brown coat that he was wearing when captured. Or you may believe, as some do, that he lay
up in some remote Polden village and ultimately escaped, while
a loyal officer sacrificed himself on the scaffold, impersonating
the duke in noble Sydney Carton fashion.

Before they rode on, Dr Oliver took the dashing plume of
black feathers from Monmouth's hat because it made him conspicuous. He carried it with him for a good part of his own
escape journey and the Oliver family in Bath handed it down as

an heirloom, until it passed to a museum in Queen Square where now, bedraggled and thinned, it is kept in a box at Bath Reference Library buildings.

Monmouth's possible routes from Sedgemoor to Hampshire are a subject for dispute and stories of the journey are too numerous to be told in full. However, some contend that he rode along the north side of the Poldens instead of the south and stayed a night at the manor house at Catcott. This house was long called Tarry House, or by some people Tally House; for years it lay in ruins and, in the present century, was used as the barn of a farm. Lately rebuilt to make a new house, it lies in a corner of Tarry Field, or Church Field, in which Catcott church is situated and most pleasantly approached by a path close to great field trees. Catcott is reached by an unclassified road off the A39 from Glastonbury to Bridgwater. At one time a boundary stone wall from Tarry House to the road contained alcoves with stone seats where people conjectured that pilgrims once 'tarried'! But for years the ancient ruined house, frequented by bats and owls, created an eerie atmosphere in the dusk or moonlight as a headless man was known to haunt it and to wander about the field at night.

The Somerset houses where Monmouth is said to have spent a night before or after the Battle of Sedgemoor are numerous, and some geographically impossible. One of these is the fine, old grey stone farmhouse, Castleman's Hill Farm, that stands on top of Castleman's Hill in the Blackdowns, halfway between Taunton and Wellington—quite a distance from Sedgemoor. Yet here some years back a carved bed was displayed in which the duke slept before the battle. And here also is a 'king's bedroom' where it is suggested 'King' Monmouth eluded the searchers by hiding between rafters and chimney. Major Tomlin, who lived at this historic house in 1882, presented a painted drum to the County Museum from which it has now been removed. It bore the arms of the Risdon family, and tradition held that it came from the field of Sedgemoor.

'God bless you, sir. I shall never see you more.' Young Dr Oliver, with tears in his eyes, pressed Monmouth's hand before spurring his horse and riding towards Bristol. They had ridden twenty miles and summer daylight was upon them when he urged Monmouth to make for Uphill, near Weston-super-Mare, and take a ferry for Wales. Through Lord Grey's persuasion the duke refused.

William Oliver, a Cornishman, was twenty-five years old and life was sweet. He had thrown up his medical studies in Leyden to go adventuring with Monmouth who made him one of the three surgeons in his army. Now he went into hiding at the home of some Bristol friends. When the Bloody Assize ended, he travelled by coach to London, calmly chatting with a travelling-companion who was Judge Jeffreys' clerk. Thankfully he returned to his studies in Leyden. One would have thought that never again would he venture to support an outside claimant to the English throne, but he came back to England with William of Orange who created him physician to the Fleet, to the Hospital for Seamen at Chatham and at the Sailors' Hospital in Greenwich. He died a bachelor in 1716. Several of these facts are recorded in black lettering on the slab commemorating.

William Oliver MD FRS

on the south wall of Bath Abbey where he is buried. The memorial inscription extols his services to King William but makes no mention of his adventures as a rebel. Yet on the pediment of the slab the sculptor carved a single curled feather.

Oliver's love for the city of Bath is evident in his writings, as the memorial inscription states, but he never seems to have practised there. The more famous Dr Oliver, who made the original Bath Oliver biscuit for his patients and made his coachman Atkins rich by bequeathing him the recipe as he lay dying, is said to have been William Oliver's illegitimate son. William Oliver himself wrote a long Dissertation on Bath Waters and, incidentally, another work setting down a case-history that

112

became a legend of the village of Timsbury.

He called it *An Account of the Extraordinary Sleeper at Timsbury*; the sleeper being Samuel Chilcot, aged twenty-five, a strong, healthy farm-labourer who, several times over, fell asleep for *months* at a time, sometimes while eating, with a pot of ale in his hand. When he woke he rose, dressed, ate normally, went straight back to his farm work but stayed silent another month. On the first occasion he slept from April till August and when he roused and went back to the fields became aware of the phenomenon only when, like a minor Rip van Winkle, he noticed that the fields where he was sowing barley just before he fell asleep were standing ready for harvest.

The people of Timsbury and neighbouring villages, even from Bath about eight miles away, came to stare at sleeping Samuel Chilcot as if he were a peep-show, and doctors arrived, uninvited, to prod and investigate, establishing that he was no fraud. Dr Oliver himself took the unwarrantable liberty of putting fiery Sal Ammoniac up Chilcot's nose, then cramming powder of white hellebore up his nostrils, so that his nose swelled and blistered. Mr Woolmer, a Bath apothecary, entered the cottage one day and bled Chilcot profusely when the poor anxious mother was absent. Another medico ran a pin into his arm as far as the bone, but Samuel Chilcot did not feel it. Once Dr Oliver managed to pour a little red Spanish wine through a hole his pipe had made in his teeth. Samuel Chilcot survived it all.

A few days after the battle Monmouth was captured, dressed as a shepherd, lying in the shade of great oak trees near the New Forest and hidden in a ditch covered by tall, thickly-growing bracken. For many years Exmoor children played a little game called the Bracken-Fern Game in which they would slice the stem of the bracken to see the 'oak' visible in its green tissues. This they called 'King Monmouth's oak'. Then they acted the part of Monmouth lying in the ferns under the oak and aimlessly cutting a fern-stem until the flash of his diamond ring betrayed

113

him to the eye of a village woman on the common who sent a search-party to take him.

Monmouth died his cruel death on 15 July; instantly there sprang up a legend that by its very character had to wane with the passage of time yet survived for many years. Somerset people in their scores, including some of Monmouth's fighting-men who had escaped or been pardoned, asserted that Monmouth was not dead, only withdrawn to Holland until the harvest was gathered in; then he would return and lead them to victory. There had been five men strongly resembling the duke, they said, and all five had sworn never to betray their true identity. One of these had been beheaded on Tower Hill for his leader's sake. One of Monmouth's ladies had had the coffin opened, looked intently at the right arm for a familiar mark and exclaimed, 'No! 'Tis not he!' People remember the story that on his death-bed Monmouth's father, Charles II, had made his brother—now James II —swear in front of the Catholic priest, Father Hudleston, that he would never execute Monmouth whatever deed the latter committed.

For three years the belief that the duke lived in Holland or France, and that several West Country gentlemen had visited him and knew his plans for returning to Somerset with an army of foreign soldiers, attracted more and more supporters, who picked up information in taverns, alehouses, coaches, markets, from those who were 'in the know'. The excitement created by these rumours reached its peak in the spring of 1688, thanks to the activities and self-importance of a talkative man called Elias Bragg.

Bragg came from Curry Rivel, near Taunton, where he had been a servant in the house of Lady Jennings, a member of the Speke family, who entertained Monmouth. He was imprisoned in the Bridewell at Taunton after the rebellion but received a pardon. In the early part of 1688, while travelling about Devon and Somerset, he made the Ship Inn at Bridgwater one of his chief stopping-places. He was 'to be found at the Sign of the

Page 115 (*above*) The Aller Dart, Low Ham Church;
(*below*) Alfred's Fort, Burrow Bridge

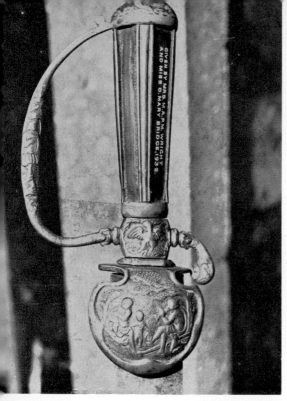

Page 116
(*left*) The Mary Bridge
Sword; (*below*) Old Barn
at Weston Court, Weston
Zoyland

Ship, Bridgwater'; there is now no such inn, although the Ship Afloat and the Ship Aground, both ancient inns, survived up to a recent date. Over their ale and cider at this inn, and in Bristol inns too, men listened open-mouthed to Bragg's tales that he had been to Holland, seen the duke, been entrusted with fifty letters for Bristol and many more for London whence carriers' carts would deliver them to various parts of the country; the letters, he said, had seals of green wax with a coat of arms displaying a unicorn, lions, three stars, and—a crown! Forty thousand men were to land in Cornwall and as many at Plymouth and Dover, while Monmouth himself would come over from Wales to Porlock and Minehead. Bragg stated that he himself had been to Bristol to find out how many cannon would be available to send to Minehead for the duke's forces. Oh yes, he added, several of the Somerset gentry would support another rising. They were constantly meeting at Mr Edward Strode's house, Downside, on Windsor Hill, a mile-and-a-half north of Shepton Mallet. Bragg's listeners all knew that Strode had entertained Monmouth, had sheltered him the first night of his flight when the duke left his pistols behind. Strode was now High Sheriff of the county, having obtained a pardon at a cost of more gold, he told his wife, Betty, than would fill her apron.

One man at the Ship, of whom Bragg made a special confidant, felt uneasy when he thought matters over, and laid information with a magistrate who promptly put him in jail for letting Bragg go on his way. However, Bragg was found, arrested, sent by the mayor to Ilchester Gaol and in April examined by two justices. He told them an elaborate and three-parts fictitious story of having been directed by an Exeter carrier to a Mr Duke's house at Otterton, Devon, when he was seeking a post as manservant. Here an ancient well-bred lady sent him to wait in the kitchen after he had told her of his service with Lady Jennings. Fifty people or more sat down to dinner and then held a religious meeting where, said Bragg, a nonconformist preacher declared in his sermon that their future deliverer, Monmouth,

117

H

was not dead and would return at midsummer. He noticed in amazement that Captain Savage, an officer in Monmouth's army and supposedly hanged at Taunton, was in the company, and Captain John Speke who had fled abroad, as well as other Somerset gentlemen who afterwards met at Downside House. When he told them that he had fought for Monmouth under Colonel Bovet of Taunton, later executed, and Captain Herring, who was hanged at Stogursey, they had hired him to carry secret letters under an oath of silence. He had confided all this and the story of Monmouth's new plot, which he could swear was true, to his friend at the *Ship* because knowledge of the plot worried him and he had not dared seek out a magistrate to hear his confession.

The Ilchester magistrates seemed rather disappointed that this sensation-monger proved 'a mere worm carrying incredible tales', and had the sense not to mete out severe punishment.

Yet how the legend of Monmouth's continued existence lingered among peasantry who took little account of dates! Hannah More, while performing her philanthropic works in the wild Mendip country of Shipham and Cheddar about a hundred and twenty years later, met rough miners who told her that one day King Monmouth would come back and put right all their wrongs.

Many stories are told of Monmouth's supernatural reappearances, of which several have been witnessed during the twentieth century. In 1924 a London journalist touring the West Country felt certain that he had seen the ghost of Monmouth. Driving his small car at midnight through heavy mist along a lonely road—and they still *were* lonely in the 1920s—running close to Sedgemoor, the journalist suddenly recalled that the misty willow-planted land on his right was the ancient battlefield where royalist soldiers defeated Monmouth's untrained army. He drove on through drifts of white vapour, along the silent road, and realised with a start that ahead of him a man was riding a big white horse of a rather heavy breed, sitting rigid, never turning his head when the car overtook him and they travelled side by side for seconds.

The driver called out some joking remark and then felt strangely chilled as he realised that the horse's hooves made no sound on the road nor when the rider turned him towards the moor and they seemed to leap a little bridge, where no bridge was, before they melted into the mist.

People swear that, in the small hours of the morning of 6 July, they have seen Monmouth and Lord Grey galloping neck and neck over the moor towards Chedzoy as they did in 1685, their horses' hooves pounding very softly on the moorland earth.

Several houses, where various legends insist that Monmouth stayed during that fateful week of July 1685, are haunted by his ghost; and even when such a house has undergone alteration some supernatural presence is still sensed by certain visitors. A notable example is Sydenham Manor, the Tudor house to which Rafael Sabatini, in his novel, brought Captain Dr Peter Blood, in the small hours after the battle of Sedgemoor, to minister to a severely wounded gentleman, only to be captured as a rebel by Colonel Kirke's dragoons. Sabatini set this house 'one mile south of Bridgwater on the right bank of the river'. The A39 road to Bath that passes it was the causeway along which Monmouth led his troops from the Castle Feld. Although historians state that Monmouth lodged in the semi-ruined Bridgwater Castle, tradition holds that he spent part of the night of 5 July at Sydenham Manor. The house is now a component of the British Cellophane complex and used as a clubhouse for some of the management personnel and for guests. The Monmouth Room, or Monmouth's bedroom, where his portrait hangs, faces eastward and when he slept in it the view embraced open Sedgemoor. Opening out of this room was the small closet where he knelt to say his prayers; now a bathroom, it retains the lancet windows. Monmouth's was the shadowy presence haunting this room and the little closet when Sydenham Manor was a private house. The iron bars of the bedroom window with its arch-headed lights were removed not long ago, and a big pear tree grows outside it where Monmouth saw a venerable oak spread its boughs. This oak was the subject of a curious little story about a member of the Perceval family, living there in the century after Monmouth's time, who was carried by some invisible spirit out of the chamber beyond his window-bars and, by levitation, set in the oak's branches.

The Bull family, who had bought Sydenham Manor in 1613, must have kept Monmouth's visit secret, for during the Civil War they had earned a reputation as firm royalists. Perhaps this reputation saved the life of Henry Bull's foolish servant the morning after the Sedgemoor battle, when exhausted rebels were beaten like hares out of the ripening corn and runaways overtaken. Henry Bull lived in the manor house at Shapwick on the peat moors, reached by turning left at the 'Shapwick' sign off the A39 after leaving Bridgwater. Now part of Millfield School, it is a fine stone building, asymmetrical, with gables and two-storeyed porch, and balustraded walls adorned with obelisks enclosing the forecourt. At this house Henry Bull planned to entertain friends to dinner on 6 July. News of the battle had not reached him. He sent his liveried servant to buy fish in Bridgwater where the man stopped to stare at red-coated soldiers, at little crowds on the bridge, at groups of fugitives and weeping relatives. During a round-up, troops arrested him while he stood gaping at some captured rebels and hauled him before Lord Feversham, who had started his summary hangings. Feversham recognised the Bull livery and accepted the terror-stricken man's explanation, telling him in biting tones to bid his master not to hang his livery again on the shoulders of such a fool. 'Go home, thou art not worth the hanging.' Perhaps he had a useful alibi in his basket of fish from the quayside near the old stone bridge. Shapwick church contains imposing monuments to the Bull family, including a very ornate one to the Henry Bull of Monmouth's day who died in 1691. The slate slab has a long beautifully-lettered Latin inscription. The sculptor added pilasters with Corinthian capitals, skulls and cross-bones, a gilded shield, and fine heraldic bulls painted scarlet.

And the other poor Sedgemoor ghosts? The wind carries the cries of the wounded on the battle-night 5–6 July, when people in the lonelier farmhouses hear the galloping of phantom horses. A stranger bought a Sedgemoor farm and in the darkness of the summer night was astonished to hear so many horses clattering down the lonely lane outside his gate. His dog rushed out barking, and when he followed he saw nothing but could hear the sound of galloping hooves fading in the distance, while the dog whined uneasily. Next day he learned that this was the night of the year when the Sedgemoor riders are heard.

Many will vouch for having seen the White Lady drifting round the site of the great grave mound, trailing her white draperies and moaning, waving her arms above her head with its flowing hair, before falling across the mound-site in a transport of grief. It is generally a night when white mist swirls about the moor. She is the girl who lost her reason and died of sorrow when Feversham hanged her lover on the Bussex Tree, where the first captured rebels swung—several of them in chains. Her lover was the champion Sedgemoor runner, who was promised his freedom if he could demonstrate his prowess. He was roped naked to a wild moorland colt and together they ran towards Brentsfield Bridge, where the runner collapsed with bleeding feet after covering three-quarters of a mile at amazing speed. He did not get his expected reprieve.

Charles Causley wrote his moving ballad 'The Song of Samuel Sweet' about this man:

> O Captain, I am waiting
> By the empty tree
> As your horde of fire
> Comes blazing on the lea.
>
> See my feet are bloody,
> With salt my eyes are blind,
> For Captain, I have left you
> Far, far behind.
>
> Why do you frown, Captain,
> As I bend the knee,
> Nor tell your tossing troopers
> That I may go free?

Jan Swayne of Moorlinch, the champion leaper, was more fortunate. A rustic rebel dragged out of his bed, he was taken at daybreak along the road to Bridgwater for hanging, followed by weeping wife, children and friends. He persuaded some stupid troopers to untie his legs and let him show his children how he could leap. Three immense leaps into the then-swampy oakwoods of Loxley Woods carried him to a safe hiding-place. Today, when some of these lovely bluebell-filled woods have been felled, you may still find, a little way off the A39, but with difficulty among the bracken, the four stones called Swayne's Leaps set up to commemorate his feat.

One more ghost legend centres on the crossroads called Claylands Corner on the Bridgwater–Stogursey road at the place where a branch-road to Nether Stowey runs in. People say that the roads round about are haunted by the ghost of a ragged soldier, 'a soldier from Sedgemoor'. They had been saying it— and seeing him—for about 250 years before workmen had to dig a hole for the signpost in the triangular grass-patch where it now stands. Only six inches below the surface they found the bones of a tall man—the remains of the soldier whose troubled spirit haunts this bit of Somerset countryside, ten miles or so from the battlefield. As the ghost wears a red coat, the soldier must have been one of those who deserted to join Monmouth, and was hanged by Colonel Kirke at the crossroads.

Several stories of treasure originated with the Monmouth Rebellion. In 1815 a farmer called Poole was tenant of a farm at Pitminster, near Taunton. One of his children dropped a knife on the farmhouse stairs where it dropped through a small hole in the woodwork. Poole's wife made the hole larger to recover her knife and, as she peered in, saw the dull gleam of brass nails. She called her husband in fright, fearing that a coffin lay under the stairs. He removed some of the staircase and uncovered a wooden coffer hidden close to the wall. It was studded with brass nails and had two locks : a military chest, in fact. When opened it revealed a quantity of gold coins that included a number of *louis d'or* from

France. Local opinion maintained that this was the Duke of Monmouth's chest, holding money for prosecuting a wider campaign. Yet some quote an alternative but very similar legend, that a farmer at Blagdon, in the Blackdown Hills, was digging in a field when he felt his spade strike something hard. This turned out to be a military chest full of gold valued at £20,000, including *louis d'or* and gold coins from Portugal. This too is supposed to be Monmouth's war-chest, hidden in 1685; and because he did not know its whereabouts his rebellion met with failure.

At Hinton Charterhouse, in the Mendips, a well-to-do yeoman family was said to owe its prosperity to the fact that one of Monmouth's officers left a valise full of money on the premises and never returned to claim it.

Two miles beyond North Petherton on the A38 from Bridgwater to Taunton, a lefthand turn leads to a lane, a lodge-gate and the drive of Leversdown Farm. The house was built early in the nineteenth century, but much older outbuildings at neighbouring Bullonshay are said to have belonged to an earlier farmhouse at Leversdown. This older farmhouse had stood for several centuries, and a great amount of gold and gold jewellery had been hidden there after the Monmouth rebellion. When every nook and cranny had been searched without success for this treasure, the owner, William Harrison, had the building rased to the ground, the foundations examined, and much of the rubble sifted; but nothing was found.

Among the many traditional treasure stories that persist are tales of 'silver down a well' somewhere in Catcott, of money hidden in old houses at Wellington and treasure belonging to George Plumley executed for joining the rising, which was buried in the grounds of Locking manor house, near Weston-super-Mare. Plumley, who owned this house, had two sons who fought for Monmouth. In the terrible days that followed the battle one of them was hanged and the other imprisoned. A search was made for Plumley who hid in a little wood near the manor-house. Just when the royalist soldiers were about to abandon their task Plumley's little white dog rushed to the wood, known for many years after as Plumley's Coppice, and barked with such joyful excitement that the troops found his master and dragged him away to be hanged on a great elm near Lockinghead. His wife gave a wild shriek, picked up the dog, and threw herself down the well in the manor-house garden. For two hundred years after, numerous people asserted that they had seen a ghostly lady glide down the garden-walk at twilight, clasping a little white dog in her arms. She vanished when she reached the two yews near the well.

Fresh from the executions and their accompanying barbarities at Weston Zoyland and Bridgwater, Colonel Kirke rode on to Taunton with two cartloads of men whose wounds had not been dressed, and a double file of marching prisoners, chained together in twos and guarded by soldiers with naked swords. Kirke's thirteen-week period of command until Judge Jeffreys arrived was filled with the execution of rebels, and any who had aided them, under martial law, without trial, and with such appalling cruelty that his stay in Taunton bequeathed a legacy of dark and blood-steeped legends which time has hardly begun to dissipate. He was aided by his notorious regiment of 'Lambs', returned from service in Tangiers, who camped on ground west of the castle known afterwards by the name of Tangier.

Kirke put up at the White Hart Inn not very far from where today the Tudor House (now called the Tudor Tavern) stands at the angle of Fore Street and High Street. The White Hart, a gabled, timbered inn which made part of a fine and historic line of buildings, was greatly altered some years ago to make a grocery store and has since been demolished for supermarket development. Kirke and his officers watched the executions from the inn balcony, sometimes in an interlude during dinner. Thirty of the rebels were hanged in batches of ten and, while their legs jerked convulsively, Kirke ordered troops to beat drums and sound the trumpets 'that they may have music for their dancing'. He and his officers drank a toast to the king during the hanging of the first batch, another to the queen during the second, and another to the Lord High Chancellor Jeffreys during the third.

Nine of the executed men were buried in the churchyard of St James's Church, where the register records each name with a note that he was 'executed for treason against the king's majesty'. One man was 'hanged' three times; that is, he was cut down twice and asked whether he would serve Monmouth if he had his time over again. With incredible defiance, he twice gasped that he would and ended by hanging in chains. Another man thought himself reprieved when his rope broke, but a ring-rope was fetched from a horse on Taunton Cornhill, where a great crowd watched the terrible spectacle, the men's relatives and friends among them. One wonders how they stood their ground to watch the ghastly quarterings, disembowellings and seethings of limbs in pitch, over fires that filled the hot August air with smoke combined with the stench of pitch. A story is told of an unfortunate ploughman who was pressed into carrying out much of the seething; some say he came from the village of Chedzoy and his surname was Napper, but whatever it was people knew him afterwards by the graphic sobriquet of Tom Boilman and made a pariah of him. They thought it a fitting end when years later in a North Petherton field he deserted his plough during a violent thunderstorm to shelter beneath an oak where lightning struck him dead.

A very beautiful girl called Lucas came to Kirke—from Crewkerne, some say, but other places are named—to implore mercy for her lover. He promised her the young man's life if she would spend the night with Kirke at the White Hart and surrender her virginity. She complied. Next morning he led her to the window, drew back the curtain and showed her her lover's body hanging from the inn-sign.

A girl crossed the reeking market-square to the White Hart entrance one morning, when the carts were already drawn up with twenty men assembled in them with nooses round their necks. She was not yet thirteen, but serious and intellectually mature for her age, of considerable beauty and dressed in white.

The crowd parted to let her through, murmuring words of pity, for many of them recognised her. She was Elizabeth Singer, come to plead for her condemned brother. Under her married name Elizabeth Rowe, she was later to publish a large number of hymns and much religious verse. The daughter of a nonconformist minister from Frome, who had been thrown into Ilchester Gaol for his religious opinions, Elizabeth was born in Ilchester but she was buried like her father in the Rook Street Congregational meeting-house at Frome, built in 1707. At the age of twelve she wrote verse, and excelled in music and drawing. She was acquainted with French and Italian, because Lord Weymouth of Longleat took great interest in this talented child and asked his chaplain, Bishop Ken, to give her lessons. Ken became her great friend and strengthened her religious life.

She came now to Kirke and amazingly her appeal touched him. He turned to a young Lieutenant Bush standing beside him on the balcony to watch the mass hanging and ordered, 'Go and direct the hangman to cut him down'. Because Kirke inspired fear, or because it was imperative to hurry, the lieutenant did not ask the reprieved man's name but went quickly to the hangman and ordered, 'You are to cut him down'. 'Him? Which him? There are twenty,' growled the hangman, indicating the men already tied to the gallows.

The boy Singer, like several of his companions, had his eyes shut while he prayed aloud. Another man snatched at this chance of life. 'It's me! Me!' he exclaimed to the executioner, who cut his rope without further question. The man fled into the crowd and escaped, while Elizabeth Singer's brother died.

The story of Mary Bridge's sword is less gloomy. The Bridges lived at Weston Zoyland in a house called Weston Court. After the battle, it became known for a time as Monmouth House, and later Verney Farm, which was almost entirely destroyed by fire many years ago. A newer house, called Court Farm, occupies the same site behind a wall opposite Weston Zoyland church and retains an interior archway of Ham stone from the old house. In

the church there are pieces of medieval glass, found lying on the
floor of the burnt ruins, displaying the shields of Seymour, Sydenham and other local families. Not far away is the inn, then called
the Three Greyhounds, where a number of royalist soldiers were
quartered, drank freely and, according to local belief, sharpened
their swords on the stone fireplace that still exists. Now renamed
the Sedgemoor Inn, it has been given an appropriately pictorial
sign.

Lord Feversham, the royalist commander-in-chief, chose Weston Court as his headquarters and the Bridges, willy-nilly, had to
offer hospitality. At supper there he was served junket from a
very beautiful dish known for two hundred years as the Feversham
Dish. Macaulay mentioned it. This dish stayed for over thirty
years in the Somerset County Museum at Taunton, displayed in
the Hall of the Bloody Assizes until sold at Christie's for seventy-
six guineas in 1902. A beautiful specimen of Hispano-Moresque
ware, about twenty inches in diameter and shallow, it was creamy-
brown overlaid with golden lustre; decorated in yellowish brown
with an eagle on an escutcheon, and bordered with a design of
flowers and ears of corn. In the nineteenth century a Weston
Zoyland woman traced descent from a grandmother's grandmother who served the junket!

One day Feversham had left this house to occupy himself with
summary executions of prisoners and Kirke had left his quarters
at the vicarage—on the site of the present Georgian vicarage—to
go to Taunton. A troop of soldiers availed themselves freely of
the hogsheads of cider, which bore the names of farmers from
Ashcott, Shapwick, Weston Zoyland and Moorlinch, who had
obsequiously supplied them. At the same time Richard Alford,
the churchwarden—whose gravestone dated 1694 is in the nave
floor of Weston Zoyland church and who seems to have shown
kindness to some of the wounded prisoners lying all night under
that magnificent carved roof—took cider out to some of these
soldiers, taking care to carry it in a jug decorated with the king's
head. Flushed with drink, a band of soldiers invaded Weston

Court and found the women of the family alone, sitting in the parlour opening out of the hall and trembling a little because of the terrifying scenes in their peaceful village. A swaggering, tipsy soldier made a grossly insulting suggestion to Mary Bridge's mother and was about to use force when Mary, aged twelve, snatched his sword from his belt and stabbed him to the heart so that he dropped dead. They took her under military escort to Colonel Kirke at the White Hart, Taunton, where she faced a court-martial. Kirke gave her an honourable acquittal, presenting her with the sword as a family heirloom, which it did indeed become, passing down from one Mary Bridge to another. Miss Mary Bridge, of Old Court, Bishop's Hull, near Taunton, who showed it to the Somerset Archaeological Society in 1862, had a personal seal inscribed 'Mary Bridge 1685' with the design of a sword over the inscription.

The Mary Bridge Sword, as it is labelled, is a short weapon resembling a dirk. It is exhibited in the Blake Museum, Bridgwater, to which it was presented by Mrs Wright and Miss Mary Bridge in 1932.

'Jeffreys breathed death like a destroying angel and sanguined his very ermines with blood.' The Lord Chief Justice, concerning whom these words were written, was for those who saw him on his western circuit, and for their descendants ever after, a fire-breathing dragon swimming in his victims' gore, a monster drunk with slaughter. In Dorset and Devon, and especially in Somerset, the image has never changed, in spite of attempts at whitewashing it by explanations that Jeffreys only interpreted with special harshness the barbarous penal code of his times and that the hideous cleaving and quartering of hanged bodies; the plucking out and public burning of hearts and bowels; the boiling of limbs in pitch and impaling of limbs and heads on poles and buildings; or the suspending of bodies in iron frameworks to rot like carrion and serve as horrible prolonged warnings, were the usual concomitants of traitors' executions. No matter. The West Country had never

128

lived through a season of such horror and came to regard its
creator, who roared ferociously at the victims he was determined
to sentence, as a creature too monstrous to be human. In Somerset
the memory of this man was so indelibly printed that stories of
his visit have been repeated and embellished for three centuries.

The Somerset trials were conducted at Wells and in the Great
Hall of Taunton Castle, which still retained its moat and draw-
bridge. The Great Hall, now part of the County Museum, was
used for the assizes until 1858. For Jeffreys' visit it was draped
with crimson hangings, and, until its museum days, retained on
its dais the chair Jeffreys occupied, one of Charles II's period,
with leather seat and back, and a spiral rail in front. At one time
this chair went to Nailsea Court near Bristol.

Numerous stories are told about the Bloody Assize of September 1685, when many of the accused were brought to Taunton
and Wells in carts from such prisons as the notorious Ilchester
Gaol. Some had wounds and fractures received in the battle,
some suffered from fever and nearly all were dirty and untended.

The Spekes of Whitelackington near Ilminster were one of the
few landed Somerset families who supported Monmouth's cause.
George Speke, an opponent of Popery, James II and Tory politics,
was a truculent and argumentative man who encouraged various
rebellious elements to meet at his house, swore that he could raise
40,000 men and entertained Monmouth himself with lavish
hospitality and flattery. The lack of weighty material aid from
this family greatly disappointed Monmouth, yet their involve-
ment was sufficient to bring them within Jeffreys' terrible orbit.
Prudently absent from the Ilminster neighbourhood at the time
of the rebellion, George Speke still had to buy his safety with a
tremendous fine. His daughter, Lady Jennings, who lived at Curry
Rivel, near Taunton, also paid to escape execution, after being
kept prisoner in her own house under the local constable's super-
vision; although she pleaded that she had only supplied a few
horses to Monmouth's men without any choice in the matter.
She lived in the Tudor mansion a mile west of Curry Rivel called

Burton Pynsent, now almost completely demolished; it passed as a gift to William Pitt, who built the folly tower of Burton Steeple. Speke and Jennings tombs can be seen in Curry Rivel church, including a monument showing baby-twins and baby-triplets in stone beds.

George Speke's elder son, John, served as one of Monmouth's captains and brought a troop of raggedly-equipped horsemen from Chard to Taunton. He escaped death by flight overseas and in the next reign became MP for Taunton. It was the younger son, Charles, on whom the frightful penalty fell and who had done far less to deserve it than other members of the family.

Charles Speke was visiting his parents for a week when they threw open their park to Monmouth and thousands of his followers. Monmouth was feasted with their own family and various Somerset gentry under the great chestnut tree all through a summer's day. [On Ash Wednesday 1887 lightning destroyed the top of this tree—but its lower part remained green.] The young Speke son served the royal visitor with due courtesy. When the duke rode through the crowded flower-strewn streets of Ilminster, Charles Speke took off his hat and 'made obeisance', whereupon Monmouth graciously leaned down to shake the boy's hand.

This, said Judge Jeffreys at his trial, marked approval of the duke's cause; besides, the prisoner—captured on his way to London—was a Protestant Dissenter. He condemned him to execution and all the revolting after-treatment. All who heard stood aghast, for this charming, courteous, gentle boy was greatly loved. A young Guards lieutenant who had been one of his escort ventured to remark to Jeffreys, 'My lord, there are two brothers. Should not this one be favoured?' Jeffreys retorted flintily, 'No, for his family owes a life. He shall die for his namesake.' The Mayor of Taunton, though far from tender-hearted, also pleaded for mercy to be shown.

At one point Charles Speke was offered a chance of pardon if he would inculpate Edmond Prideaux, swearing that he and other gentlemen had drunk Monmouth's health at dinner and that Prideaux had later supplied the duke with mounted men. Edmond Prideaux was master of Forde Abbey, the lovely Ham-stone house on the Somerset–Dorset border which was coveted by Jeffreys. Situated four miles south-east of Chard, it is open to the public. Speke firmly refused to give such evidence and was bravely backed-up by an Ilminster clothier who had also attended the dinner. Jeffreys sentenced Speke to die at Ilminster, where they hanged him from a great tree in the market-place. The streets of the ancient town, beneath that magnificent church-tower, were packed with anguished sightseers pressing round to touch him, to bless him, many weeping and offering to die in his stead. He prayed for an hour and sang a hymn before his death while the crowd's lamentations nearly drowned his voice. Charles Speke died with dignity and without rancour.

Another old Somerset family, the Bovets, were deeply impli-cated in the rebellion and met tragic punishment. The family, who lived at Wellington, had fought for Cromwell and garrisoned the house—built by the celebrated Lord Chief Justice, Sir John Popham—against the king. In Cromwell's time they had received Milverton lands taken from the royalist Sir John Stawell of Cothelstone Manor, whose Tudor house of red sandstone had been reduced to half-ruin by Blake; very skilfully restored, this house can be seen at the end of an avenue of young aspens that leads also to the little red sandstone church at the bottom of Cothelstone Hill.

At the time of the Bloody Assize, a Lord Stawell lived in a mansion at Low Ham, but he happened to be staying in his dilapidated manor-house at Cothelstone and, in spite of his royal-ist sympathies, refused to entertain Jeffreys, whose barbarities appalled him. To teach him a salutary lesson, Jeffreys decreed that Colonel Richard Bovet and Thomas Blackmore should be hanged at Cothelstone; it is not certain whether their bodies swung from the battlements of that beautiful gatehouse, with its shell-shaped niches, at the top of the avenue or from the stone gateposts close to the roadway, beneath the Quantocks and shadowed by beeches. Bovet's sons, Philip and Edmond, were two of Monmouth's captains. Edmond was condemned but 'respited' or transported; while Philip met his death at Wellington with two other men, all three being hanged on a cob-walled lin-hay, or stable, next to the White Hart Inn in the High Street. This linhay became known as Gallows House, just as the hill where the Dunster rebels, Henry Lackwell, John Geans and William Sully were hanged is still called Gallox Hill; the pack-horse bridge they had to cross to climb up its slope is called Gallox Bridge, their gibbets, or perhaps a tree, standing south of the road to Timberscombe.

Colonel Bovet's young daughter, Katherine, had walked in the procession of pupils from Miss Blake's school, and the uncertainty of her fate must have been a crowning anguish for her father. At Yeovil a man called Bernard Thatcher was executed for bravely concealing Colonel Bovet before his arrest.

Up till 1864 when it was felled for road extensions, Chard possessed a splendid old oak tree with a forty-foot span, called the Gallows Oak or Hang Cross Tree. Twelve Chard rebels were sent from Taunton Assizes to be hanged on this tree on 30 September 1685 (while twelve more were hanged at Dorchester). Among them, with John Bunyan's son-in-law James Durnett, was Monmouth's very faithful manservant, William Williams, who had several narrow escapes after the battle and actually brought back to an astonished owner a horse that at some time had been lent to the duke. In the hour of defeat he was seen carrying the duke's cloak 'with ye starr on it'. When taken he still had a purse containing 200 guineas belonging to Monmouth, whom he had hastily furnished with 100 guineas at the moment of flight. The duke had put some of the gold coins inside his gold snuff-box, which, with some of the guineas, were found by Monmouth's captors and two or three informers received a share. Williams died with remarkable heroism, refusing to give any information about people who had helped his master.

Caption John Hucker was one of Monmouth's most prominent officers, although never completely trusted. He was an adventurous type, newly married at the time of the rebellion. On a June day he came riding into Taunton from Chard in command of a troop of horse—the first of Monmouth's forces to enter the welcoming town, where Monmouth would have himself proclaimed king at the market cross. Captain Hucker was a very prosperous merchant in the serge-making trade, but had engaged in other ventures that included some tentative development of a Mendip silver-mine. He was a churchwarden, had been made constable of Taunton, and hoped Monmouth would make him governor of the town during the coming struggle. Accordingly he gave the duke the use of his Taunton house as headquarters. This house stood in East Street, exactly opposite the Three Cups Inn, which occupied the site of the present County Hotel. Here Monmouth received his visitors and had consultations with his officers, some of whom always disliked Captain Hucker. The captain owned another house, a farmhouse he had built on the isle of Athelney, using the stones of the ruined abbey, which he had bought and demolished.

Hucker's ambition to be governor was frustrated by Monmouth's refusal to garrison Taunton, but he rode to Sedgemoor field in command of a troop. There, as he stood in darkness and marsh-mist on the Langmoor Stone by Langmoor Rhine that had halted the rebels, he treacherously fired the fatal pistol-shot that sent a royalist sentry galloping off with shouts of 'Sound the alarm!' Monmouth exclaimed at his perfidy; another officer swore he would kill him. The day after the battle Hucker gave himself up, fearing that women relatives of prisoners would tear him to pieces and counting on not being convicted. In Taunton Bridewell he was in danger of lynching. Yet, when he came up before Jeffreys and pleaded that he had fired his pistol to warn the king's army, Jeffreys replied that he was therefore a traitor to both king and duke, and deserved a double death. A number of Taunton people vainly interceded for him, and before his execution he wrote to a friend to repudiate the act of betrayal: 'I

133

J

also lye under a reproach of being unfaithful to an interest that I owned, which I utterly deny.'

He died very bravely but with his name tarnished. Little Eliza Hucker, who was related to him, was waiting to be ransomed from the danger of transportation as she was another of the Taunton Maids from Miss Blake's school and had presented an embroidered flag to Monmouth at Captain Hucker's house.

In Taunton, hangings took place on what was called Cornhill, the gibbets standing where we see the Market House. Here a great fire was kindled so that condemned men from the Bride-well, passing it on their way to death, would see where their bowels would burn. Young Benjamin Hewling was one of these. He was the twenty-two-year-old son of a rich London merchant, good-looking, well-educated, of engaging personality, a devout Baptist yet a light-hearted, amusing companion. He became a member of Monmouth's special bodyguard, and when he landed with him at Lyme, the duke made him captain of a troop of horse. At the same time Monmouth conferred a lieutenancy on Benjamin's brother William who, at nineteen, left his boarding-school —where both brothers had gone after their father's death—to throw in his lot with Monmouth. The duke, in their opinion, stood 'for English liberties and the Protestant religion'. On the battle-night Benjamin was absent, having taken a detachment of his men to fetch cannon from Minehead. Returning to find rout, confusion and terror, he fled with his brother and put out to sea, but had to return as their boat was in danger of being wrecked on the rocks. In Devon, where there were many troops, they surrendered to a gentleman, and were sent to Exeter Gaol, then by boat to London. There they were put in irons and parted, William being sent to Dorchester, Benjamin to Taunton. Before he reached the age of twenty, William was hanged with others on Lyme beach, where a few weeks earlier they had landed full of hope and zest for adventure. His body was spared the indignity of quartering, which meant that his family had paid a high price. Some young girls of Lyme had the courage to bear him to a

134

grave in the south-west corner of the churchyard. In prison, and
to his end, his fortitude and unshaken faith caused everyone to
marvel.

Hannah Hewling, their sister (who was later to marry Cromwell's grandson), wrote to their mother, 'My brother Benjamin
expects not long to continue in this world and is exceeding willing to leave it when God shall call but there is still room for
prayer for one.' She threw all her strength into trying to save
Benjamin's life and even obtained an audience to petition James
II who, as Churchill—later Duke of Marlborough—warned her,
proved to have a heart as hard as a marble mantelpiece. In
Taunton she ran after the Lord Chief Justice's coach, clinging
frantically to the wheel with her hands, while imploring him to
respite Benjamin's execution a mere two days in return for £100.
Jeffreys ordered the coachman to whip her fingers from the wheel.
In the darkness and despair of the prison, Benjamin's heroic
faith shone like a light. He tirelessly comforted his doomed companions with the promise of immortality and never wavered when
told overnight of his imminent death. With his fellows he was
drawn on a sledge to the gibbet on the last day in September.
The horses stubbornly refused to pull the vehicle—as was also
reported about William's last journey—so that the enraged sheriff
and officers had to lend their physical aid. Crowds of weeping
mourners filled the streets and wondered at Benjamin's cheerful
countenance. Hannah had seen him in the prison and told his
friends that he had smilingly made her read to him the chapter
from the Epistle to the Corinthians that affirms 'we have a house
. . . not made with hands'. At the execution place the prisoners
embraced and Benjamin Hewling requested permission to pray
aloud. The surly sheriff replied, 'Will you pray for the king?'

'I pray for all men', said Hewling, and afterwards asked leave
for the condemned company to sing a psalm. The sheriff brutally
told him that it must be with ropes about their necks. They
accepted the condition and sang with such fervour that a specta-
tor recorded, 'It both broke and rejoiced hearts.' An army officer

who had predicted that these men would quickly change their demeanour when they saw what sort of death awaited them, said after the execution: 'If you'd learn how to die, go to the young men of Taunton.'

For the enormous sum of £1,000 Benjamin's body was spared the quartering and permitted burial in the parish church of St Mary Magdelene at Taunton, where the registers, listing the burials for 1 October 1685, show the entries:

Oct 1   King's soldier
           Benjamin Hewlyn
           William Jenkins   } Rebels executed
           Henry Lisle

Horrible legends were created by the ghastly spectacle of rebels' dismembered bodies set up in streets and alongside high-ways. The rumour sprang up in Wiveliscombe that rebels' quar-ters had been 'dressed like pigs' and hung up in the butchers' stalls of the market, so that for some weeks housewives refused to buy meat there. At Crewkerne, a mob entered the East Street premises of two old brothers who were tallow-chandlers and threatened to kill them because they were suspected of buying rebels' bodies for melting down.

The deeds of one man kindled a nobler legend in the dark-ness of Ilchester Gaol, where 400 Sedgemoor prisoners awaiting trial lay in such filth in their irons, in great heat, that their untended wounds suppurated and their fevers threatened to infect the town population. An Ilchester surgeon, Dr Thomas Winter, defiantly entered this hell to tend men whose cause he despised; setting fractures, cleansing wounds, dressing burns, providing medicines and bandages, all at his own cost. The magistrates were afraid to pay for any assistance to rebels, until Dr Winter wrote to the king and humbly asked if he might receive the sum of about £35 that he had expended, since he was a poor man with 'a great family' and the town had benefited by his labours. He was not reimbursed until two years later.

In Wedmore it is said that Jeffreys ordered a doctor, who had dressed the wounds of a dying Puritan rebel, to be hanged on the market-cross near the village shambles. This stone cross was a beautiful specimen of fourteenth-century art, but in the hundred years since Pooley made drawings for his *Old Stone Crosses of Somerset* time and weather have further damaged the sculptured figures of the Virgin, the Holy Child and St John that decorated its canopied head. This cross now stands behind an iron gate and rails, at the top of some steps, in the Borough district of Wedmore.

The church of St John the Baptist, Glastonbury, has a small crucifix hanging on the wall between the Lady Chapel and the sanctuary. The cross is made of bog-oak, believed to have come from the Glastonbury peat moors; the ivory figure of Christ, of which the uncrossed and separately nailed feet suggest that it was carved not later than 1300, is considered one of the most beautiful in Europe. At some point in his Western Assize journey, Jeffreys with unconscious irony bought this crucifix that was by tradition a former possession of Glastonbury Abbey. Its subsequent history is obscure, but at one time it belonged to George IV and in later times to a descendant of the French royal family from whom a former vicar of Glastonbury acquired it.

Even after death Judge Jeffreys entered the realm of Somerset legend, and in a very curious manner. His body was buried near Monmouth's in the Chapel Royal of St Peter ad Vincula at the Tower of London, but three years later it was taken up and transferred to the family vault in St Mary's, Aldermanbury. Yet Somerset people say that the latter statement is false. Jeffreys' sister, Mary, lived at the tiny remote village of Stocklinch Ottersay, which is reached by turning north at Ilminster on to the B3168 road, and after five miles taking the unclassified road to the right, where the sign indicates Stocklinch. Mary Jeffreys knew a man from Curry Mallet named Valentine Pyne who held an official post at the Tower; and she paid him to have her brother's body put into an anonymous coffin and sent down to

Somerset. But in 1693 hideous memories of the Bloody Assize were still fresh in the mind and, when it became known in Taunton that the coffin was on its way to Stocklinch, it was broken open, the body decapitated and hung on the gallows in the market-place. In the dead of night men came to take down the trunk and carry it to Stocklinch. By lantern-light they left Taunton by way of East Reach, passing the Tudor almshouses built by Robert Gray and the older thatched Leper Hospital, and set out along the road to Curry Rivel, turned on to the present B3168, carrying their burden over the bridge at Hambridge and on through Puckington, with the low green pastures watered by the rambling little river Isle on both sides of their route. The final lane to the village from the Stocklinch turn, at that time bordered by fields of flax and hemp, now runs between hedges of blackberry and hawthorn bounding meadows and cornfields. Bungalows have sprung up in several orchards and Ham-stone barns have acquired roofs of corrugated iron. But there are still a number of stone cottages with thatch and stone houses with mullions of yellow stone, lying alongside the village street. The diminutive church of St Mary Magdalen stands on higher ground and half in a grass meadow, yet remains inconspicuous because it has no tower but only a bell-cot, whose openings reveals bells verdigris-green. It is a most charming little church, with its grey-gold stone patterned with silvery and yellow lichens and its interior adorned by an eighteenth-century musicians' gallery that has a central painted panel depicting a crowned King David and his harp. Stocklinch used to be divided into two parishes with two churches (now united). The men carried the coffin past the first, making for the church of St Mary Ottersay, which is absolutely hidden away. The visitor today must turn into a lane past the Manor Farm that resembles a private road, but bears a No Exit sign. After a few hundred yards this lane becomes wetter with streams, and is over-shadowed by beeches and sycamores; on its left side a field-gate between hollies carries a notice 'To the Church'.

It must already have been an arduous journey along rough eighteenth-century roads and miry lanes; now, from this field-gate, the group of men with their macabre burden in its lead coffin had to negotiate the long slope of the field called Lynches where the highest portion, behind the church, can be seen to drop in definite lynchets or terraces. The field has fine trees worthy of a park, but even today not even a rough path to the church. This one too is tiny, composed of a nave and small south transept where, on the sill of a lovely Decorated window, there lies the effigy of an appealing thirteenth-century lady, her head tied in a kerchief. When Jeffreys' body entered the church, this effigy lay in the cusped arched recess of the south wall of the nave. With the vicar presumably complying, Mary Jeffreys had the leaden coffin laid in the family vault beneath the floor on the south side, where the yellow Ham stone flags have been hollowed by the tread of feet. The Tudor mason who cut the inscription on the tablet under the south window spelt the name 'Jeffrey'. A memorial slab on a wall records that another Mary Jeffreys was buried in these vaults just a hundred years after the Bloody Assize year. The church owns a silver paten, made in 1705, that is engraved with the Jeffreys family crest, and the name of one of the family is inscribed on a bell.

The hill field behind the church is full of springs; in wet seasons water poured into the vaults and perhaps one spring welled up beneath. The vaults were flooded so deeply that the coffins floated about. It was said that Jeffreys' coffin, though of lead, floated too, and always with its feet towards the steps at the entrance. Two men engaged on redecorating Barrington church, near Stocklinch, in the nineteenth century, were lodging near the Royal Oak Inn at Barrington. (Barrington Court, open to the public, is the beautiful house belonging to William Strode, who entertained Monmouth on his happy progress.) One night, over pots of ale at the inn, a local labourer told them that in his boyhood he had seen the church vaults flooded and coffins floating in the water. He had held the lantern while his father, the sexton at Stocklinch, replaced the coffins, and had seen Jeffreys' lead coffin floating, foot foremost, towards the opening. This vault, which contains among other coffins one unnamed coffin of lead, was sealed in 1934.

Jeffreys' ghost treads heavily along passages and paces up and down the Great Hall of Taunton Castle at dead of night during September—the month of the Bloody Assize—and can be heard moving about the upper floor of the Tudor House in Fore Street, Taunton, whose striking timberwork of 1578 makes it one of the town's best buildings. It was the town house of the Portmans of Orchard Portman, and here Sir William Portman entertained Jeffreys to dinner in the Great Chamber that disappeared when the house ceased to be a private residence. In St Mary Street, Bridgwater, there is a timber-framed seventeenth-century building called Marycourt, or Judge Jeffreys' Lodgings, where Jeffreys stayed on a two-day journey he made between Taunton and Bristol. Though the house has become business premises and acquired plate-glass windows, on certain nights the sound of the ghostly judge's footsteps echoes hollowly down its passages and his hand knocks on the doors.

Solitary travellers have heard a spectral groan of one of Jeffreys' victims, or the creak of a rope, when they passed a Hanging Tree, such as the great Heddon Oak outside Stogumber, near Taunton. But a strange nebulous legend has been narrated about a mass ghostly appearance of executed rebels on the night of 22 September 1690, that is, at the season of the Bloody Assize but five years later.

A Mr Sealey of Taunton started to ride home from Exeter at three in the afternoon, making for the road over the Blackdown Hills. He stopped for a time to drink a pot of beer and a noggin of brandy at an inn, where many coaches, waggons and horsemen called, and found himself almost benighted after he had ridden several more miles in the Taunton direction. In the gathering darkness he met a stout friendly farmer on a grey mare, who persuaded him to ride back two or three miles to an inn that provided very good lodgings. They reached the crest of a rise in the road and saw a lonely, large house with an inn-sign just visible in the gloom. In front of it lay a big expanse of uncultivated ground. When Mr Sealey turned to speak to the farmer, he found to his surprise that he had suddenly vanished and that forty or fifty men, with a few women, were gathering round him, carrying spears with which they seemed to threaten him in silence. Very frightened, he quoted some verses of scripture. They made no answer, but wrapped his head in 'something like a fishing-net'. He alighted from his horse which laid his nose over Mr Sealey's shoulder 'like a Christian', as if seeking companionship. The ghostly figures gave a treacle-like substance to the horse, which let them lead him away, not to be seen again.

Mr Sealey, sweating with fear, walked up and down the plot of ground all night. Time and again the ghostly crowd lunged at him. He thrust at them with his sword and found 'nothing but shadow', although he saw the sad figures shake their heads at each other and weep. Ten funerals came by in a black procession, pressing close to Mr Sealey, who again used his sword but found no substance in the figures. When a grey dawn streaked the sky, he saw the piece of ground empty and the house too.

Mr Sealey set out to walk the road over the wooded Blackdowns and found the house known in later years as 'Judges' where judges from Exeter Assizes were lodging on their way to Wells. He told them his curious story, whereupon some member of the household informed them that the inn where the so-called farmer had taken him to lodge for the night had belonged to an innkeeper who joined Monmouth's men and was hanged from his own inn-sign, while the plot of land where Mr Sealey had been kept prisoner for a night was the burial-ground for a large number of the rebels. Unkind people have suggested that Mr Sealey's wanderings and strange visions were possibly due to his having drunk more ale and brandy than he stated.

Hundreds of men who joined the Monmouth Rebellion were condemned by Jeffreys to transportation to the West Indies and sold as slaves to the owners of plantations. In Somerset, up to the present century, the legend persisted that a strange colony of people existed in Barbados who were the descendants of Somerset men sold into slavery for the price of 1,500lb of sugar per head. These descendants were known as Red-Leg Johnnies because of their peculiar colour. They segregated themselves with a kind of pride, hating all negroes, including those who employed them. They were simple and ignorant, fanatical and bigoted in religion, and very poor. Physically and mentally degenerate from 250 years of inter-marriage, they had acquired a scaly skin, that reddened and freckled thickly instead of tanning, and hair and eyebrows so fair as to be nearly white. An eccentric grammar and a limited vocabulary characterised their spoken English, but they used an unmistakeable Somerset pronunciation with rich broad vowels. A surprising number of Red-leg Johnnies were fine fiddlers and a few of them knew the tunes of old Somerset songs that the first sad emigrants remembered and sang to their children in an utterly strange land.

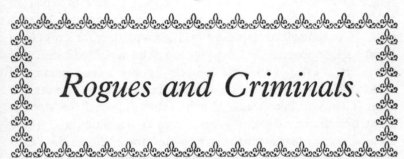

3

Rogues and Criminals

BAMPFYLDE MOORE CAREW

Bampfylde Moore Carew is traditionally known as King of the Gipsies and as King of the Beggars, but the latter is his appropriate title. True, he was once elected as their chief by a crowd of gipsies, who had much more pure Romany blood than the twentieth-century Somerset 'diddicoys', but not a drop of it ran in his veins. He was born in 1699 into an aristocratic family, the Carews, in the Devon village of Bickleigh, near the river Exe. While his own death and burial have faded into obscurity, the tombs, busts, monuments and brasses of several ancestors and relatives are to be seen in Bickleigh church and in the church at Haccombe, another South Devon village. A branch of the same family lived at Crowcombe, under the Quantocks, off the Taunton–Williton road (A358). There, in the days when Bampfylde Moore Carew was roaming Somerset as a swindling vagabond, Thomas Carew, with Ireson the Wincanton architect, built the stately house of red brick called Crowcombe Court—now sadly

143

dilapidated—with its great handsome stable-block. There is, however, no story of his visiting this Carew mansion, although he turned up several times at some of the finest country houses in the county.

A trifling event set him on the crooked path of picaresque adventure that he pursued for over fifty years. His father, the rector of Bickleigh, sent him to Blundell's School in Tiverton where they granted a certain indulgence towards pupils who took time off to follow the stag hunt and allowed them to maintain a small pack of hounds. One day a group of boys sighted a deer and set off in pursuit with their hounds. It was a long chase and eventually all gave up, except young Carew and three companions called Coleman, Escott and Martin. They followed the stag for miles over farmland and through fields of standing corn, to the fury of several farmers who complained forcefully to the headmaster. The four boys, too scared to return, ran away to lose themselves in a band of gipsies who roamed the Exmoor wilds and the rough, steeply-banked hedged lanes of Devon and West Somerset. Carew came home after a year or two, but found civilised existence far too tame and tedious. Thereafter, he adopted a vagrant's life, battening on any ordinary citizen who believed a highly coloured hard-luck story, and choosing gipsies, beggars and ne'er-do-wells as close companions. His three truant school-mates were often with him so that it seems evident that they too became wanderers and beggars, while not possessing the panache and impudence that made Carew a figure of renown and, at times, something like a hero in the eyes of his victims.

The fabulous events of the years he spent in and out of foreign countries must be summarised briefly. On his return from a short stay in Newfoundland, he posed as the mate of a vessel and married the daughter of a Newcastle apothecary. A series of frauds earned him transportation to a penal settlement in Maryland from which he escaped, only to be recaptured and restrained by a cruel iron collar. Somehow he fell into the hands of Indians who felt friendly enough towards him to remove it: Carew, when he wished, exerted charming powers of persuasion. In Pennsylvania he obtained money by pretending to be a Quaker. Back in England he was very nearly impressed into service on board a man o' war, but saved himself, so the story goes, by pricking the skin of his face and rubbing in bay salt and gunpowder to simulate smallpox. At the age of forty, he started roving about Somerset, with occasional expeditions into Dorset and Devon, maintaining himself by every trick a vagrant rascal could practise, imposing on the credulous, flattering and sponging on the rich, yet at the same time providing much amusement. He was a colourful, unpredictable, unscrupulous figure whose arrival instantly created suspicion and excitement. The West Country gipsies had elected him as king in succession to their dead leader Patch (also of West Country birth), and he boasted that he could practise every gipsy art as skilfully as any Romany. Most of his exploits were indeed the simple frauds, dressed-up in elaborate ritual, that gipsies have perpetrated down the centuries.

The village of West Monkton, dominated by a tall grey church tower, lies four miles north of Taunton just off the Taunton–Bridgwater road (A38). Here lived an ingenuous lady called Mrs Musgrave who had been told that somewhere in her garden a sum of money lay buried. She heard of Bampfylde Moore Carew's skill in necromancy and jumped eagerly to the conclusion that he could divine the whereabouts of the treasure. When he was in the neighbourhood, she sent him a message, and he walked to West Monkton down lanes whose banks were doubtless as blue with wild borage as they are today. He assured Mrs Musgrave that wealth certainly lay hidden under the earth of her garden. He read the stars, drew up her horoscope, consulted a mysterious book, then solemnly named a date when Mrs Musgrave's star would find a store of gold under a laurel-tree in her garden. Mrs Musgrave, almost tearful with delight, paid him a fee of twenty guineas, waved him good-bye and settled down to wait for the auspicious day. When it dawned she hastened out with her spade to the laurel-tree, dug for an hour, but turned up nothing more

145

valuable than a few stones. By this time Carew was over the hills and far away.

Once he went to Mr Pleydell's house at Milborne Port, a Somerset village on the edge of Dorset. He came humbly to the stable door, wearing an old stocking for a cap and a woman's ragged mantle, but no stockings or shirt. He told Mr Pleydell the touching tale that he was 'a poor castaway'; a Frenchman had taken him up, with his eight companions who, to his grief, had all drowned. Mr Pleydell had been moved to pity—especially as Carew's voice suggested that he had been born a gentleman—and gave him a suit of clothes plus a guinea. A few weeks later Carew came to the Portmans' house near Blandford, posing as a poverty-stricken ratcatcher, wearing a shaggy cap and carrying a tame rat in a box slung at his side. He was sent into the kitchen to get a free dinner. Several gentlemen in the house had met the famous impostor before, but only a parson called Bryant recognised him and revealed his identity. 'By gad sir!' exclaimed Mr Pleydell, beaming. 'I've always desired the pleasure of your acquaintance, I've heard so much about such a famous trickster, but you've never come my way before.'

Contradicting him, Carew told the company the story of Mr Pleydell's charity towards a castaway. They roared with laughter and tipped Carew handsomely. 'Never again!' swore Mr Pleydell. 'After this I'd recognise you in any guise!'

Parson Bryant slipped out to follow the departing vagrant, told him the date when they would all be dining at Mr Pleydell's and asked him to turn up again at Milborne Port. Carew only shrugged and replied that he could not promise the gentlemen.

As they wined and dined at Mr Pleydell's, the gentlemen heard a great clamour outside: the barking of dogs, the yelling of a child, the shouting of stablemen and servants. A servant told them that a destitute woman with three young children in her charge was begging for charity. They went out and found a stooping old dame, wearing a high-crowned hat over a cotton nightcap tied under her chin, whose back was burdened with two screaming

146

infants, while she carried a poor little hunchbacked child. She was their grandmother, she said, and the children were nigh starvation; their dear mother and her possessions had perished in a dreadful fire in a distant county. The gentlemen praised the old woman for her Christian charity and made generous contributions from their purses. After her departure they heard the sound of a hunting-horn and of loud halloo-ing; their dogs rushed madly out, and they thought some hunting sportsman was passing. Suddenly they remembered the old dame and—Bampfylde Moore Carew! The woman was fetched in and Carew revealed. He had borrowed the two babies and pinched them hard to make them scream, and the little hunchback had been hired from a tinker for a trifling sum. All this appealed to these eighteenth-century gentlemen's sense of horse-play. They made merry and rewarded him. Such gentlemen abetted Carew's roguery on several occasions, including Lord Weymouth at his home at Maiden Bradley, in Wiltshire, who rewarded him with ten guineas and a suit of clothes. Similarly, Sir Charles Tynte, squire of the pretty Quantock village of Goathurst, received him in the courtyard of Halswell House and, with a local parson as witness, wagered that he would never manage to delude shrewd Lady Tynte with one of his preposterous tales. However, Carew soon proved that he could, not only receiving alms from her, but, amid much mirth, also the wager and the parson's half-crown. He came on more than one occasion to this fine house built by Sir Halswell Tynte, ten years before Carew was born, and now standing forlorn and half-empty. A beggarly yet arrogant figure, he walked the long driveway through the park of magnificent trees, admired by eighteenth-century travel-writers and now so sadly felled. He saw in course of construction the miniature temples and pavilions now falling into ruin.

Carew made at least one profitable tour, in the summer of 1745, round those beautiful villages in the Yeovil neighbourhood that are built of the honey-coloured Ham stone and contain several exquisite manor-houses. At the great Elizabethan Montacute

House, he imposed on the charity of Lady Phelips with some highly original tale of woe, and encountered Parson Thomas Bowyer, of Martock, who failed to recognise him and gave him sixpence when told by Carew that he was the unfortunate brother of the nonconformist Tiverton minister, Mr Pike. Bowyer asked Mr Pike's 'brother' if he had heard any recent news of Bampfylde Moore Carew. 'What! the famous dogstealer?' exclaimed the visitor. 'They say he's dead—hanged, mostly likely.' Dog-stealing was another of Carew's activities; he could cajole animals as effectively as he could humans.

He begged hospitality of some soft-hearted spinster sisters, the Misses Hawker, who lived at Thorne, near Yeovil. They too believed his story about the Tiverton minister and sent him across the road to their local Dissenting minister. Again Carew told his tale about being brother to Mr Pike, who laboured so hard to instruct his congregation and was nearly as poor as himself. He went away expressing humble gratitude for the gift of a half-guinea to himself, and with a good holland shirt 'for Mr Pike of Tiverton'.

Parsons and squires he regarded as legitimate prey. He went to the Rev Mr White of East Coker, a lovely village, lying among trees under a hill on which the church is set alongside Coker Court, home of the Helyar family for many years. Carew was unabashed by the presence of Thomas Proctor, a rich farmer, churchwarden and magistrate from West Coker, another village with Ham-stone houses, and a beautiful small manor-house, where Thomas Proctor's son would live. Here Carew posed as an unfortunate sailor who had been shipwrecked somewhere in the Baltic and was now trying to get home to his native Tintagel. The same day he told an East Coker tanner that he was a tanner made bankrupt by dishonest customers.

Once he came to Cannington Court, the home of Lord Clifford, in the Quantock foothills, and told him a hard-luck story. He had known Lord Clifford, who came of a Devon family, during his boyhood. The Tudor house of red Quantock sandstone, built round a courtyard of irregular shape, stands close to the fine church with the lofty tower of red sandstone—faded to pink—that dominates an expanse of rural Somerset. Now used by the Somerset Farm Institute, it lies just off the A39 road, three miles from Bridgwater.

The great Bridgwater fair, called St Matthew's and still held in late September, always drew hordes of vagrants, gipsies, beggars and charlatans, of whom Bampfylde Moore Carew, who mingled with them several times, was perhaps the most famous and colour-ful. Once he staged a special parade to St Matthew's Field, hobbling on crutches, with a crew of beggarly followers all 'crippled', 'lame' or 'blind', and looking very pitiful—among them his three old Tiverton schoolfriends, Escott, Coleman and Martin. They collected a harvest of coins from the warm-hearted people who travelled from remote Somerset villages once a year to visit the fair. But shrewder observers reported their antics as fraudu-lent. The mayor, remarking that he knew a swift remedy to help the lame walk and the blind to see, had them rounded up and locked in the dark little gaol in Fore Street. A physician, real or feigned, came to advise them to hasten out of town as soon as it was daylight, because no mercy would be shown if they appeared before the magistrates. They found the doors open early and fled. The mayor and a number of people watched from a building opposite, and like the crowd in the street roared with mirth at this speedy flight of the halt, maimed and blind. Crutches, sticks and wooden legs were thrown aside. Bampfylde Moore Carew left the torn skirt of his coat in a man's detaining hand. His friend Coleman ignored the old three-arched stone bridge choked with fairgoers and swam the river Parrett. One genuinely lame beggar was brought back to the mayor, who rebuked him for vagrancy but kindly relieved his poverty.

Sometimes the degrading conditions of Carew's chosen exist-ence half-submerged him. He arrived in Bridgwater one day in August 1744 and put up at a common alehouse—its keeper's description—with two female companions. Probably he defaulted

K

on paying or perhaps his disorderly behaviour annoyed the ale-house-keeper so much that she was goaded into retaliation. In the Somerset Records Office there is a torn and faded document covered with slanting lines of hand-writing in ink that the years have turned brown. Its statement runs as follows:

> The information of Sarah Leakey of Bridgwater aforesaid was taken on oath the Twenty Second day of August 1744, before William Binford Esq. Alderman and one of his Majesty's Justices of the peace...
>
> Who saith that she now keeps a Common Alehouse within the Borough aforesaid and that yesterday about noon one Bampfylde Moore Carew came to this informant's House and desired to lodge there which he did last night, and saith that this Evening the said Bampfylde Moore Carew came into this Informant's House very Drunk and greatly intoxicated with Liquor and this Informant further saith that the said Carew hath now with him at her House, a woman whom he called his wife and a Girl his Daughter, and their Informant believes this Bampfylde Moore Carew to be a Common Strolor [sic] and hath nothing to subsist on but what gentlemen give him.
>
> Sarah Leakey
> Sworn this day and year above said Before me.
> J. W. Binford

Despite Sarah Leakey's insinuations about the women, Carew is said to have had a wife, and a daughter to whom he taught the tricks of his trade.

His end is unknown. Some say that he reformed his ways after winning a large sum of money in a lottery. Yet he had always turned a deaf ear to relatives' pleadings, even to Sir Thomas Carew, of Haccombe, who offered him a regular allowance if he would renounce the beggar's life and become respectable.

JOHN POULTER, ALIAS BAXTER

John Poulter, known alternatively as John Baxter, was one of the most notorious eighteenth-century highwaymen. To judge by advertisements raising 'the Hue and Cry' for him in contemporary newspapers like the *Western Flying Post*, he possessed many of the attributes with which novelists have endowed their highwaymen-heroes. He led a little gang of desperadoes whom he absolutely dominated; he always had several stolen horses at his disposal; women could not resist him and were as eager as their husbands were to become his accomplices; he had travelled abroad as far as Jamaica and Africa, and in many parts of England; he held up horsemen and coaches, committing his bold robberies in a dozen different counties, although Wiltshire, Somerset and part of Dorset formed his favourite hunting-ground. A tall man with a scar on his cheek, he sometimes talked French, boasting that he would introduce the French way of robbery. He swore he would never be taken alive and that he had no fear of death.

However, he *was* taken alive in Exeter, after many years of crime, and put into Exeter Gaol where his wife, also a criminal, awaited transportation to America. The 'Hue and Cry' raised for him, after his last highwayman's exploit a week earlier, had helped authority to run him to earth. On 21 March 1753 Dr Hancock—who lived in the cathedral close at Salisbury and belonged to the well-known Somerset family long resident at Lydeard St Lawrence, near Taunton, as well as at Wiveliscombe, where they built the Dispensary still seen there—set out with his little granddaughter and his manservant in a hired post-chaise to visit his wife, who was ill and taking the waters in Bath. The coach-road from Salisbury ran for its last lap across the broad and thickly wooded sweep of Claverton Down, high above the lovely valley of the Avon that cradled the city, before descending steeply to Bath by what is now the A36. To make the descent, coaches and carriages had to slow down after taking a sharp turn at the top of Brassknocker Hill, which made it a favourite place for highwaymen. John Poulter availed himself of it several times, for the Salisbury–Bath road was one of his favourite haunts. He had tolerably safe and comfortable quarters in a nest of associates in Bath where, by sometimes dealing in tea, he covered up his more deadly activities by pretending to be nothing worse than a smuggler.

That night in March, Poulter was mounted on a little bay horse and accompanied by a confederate called Burke. They attacked the post-chaise as it approached the town at nightfall, firing their pistols through the glass at the sides, and then through the back, just missing the head of the cowering child. When they fired through the front Dr Hancock made haste to alight with the child clasped in his arms. He said afterwards that the two highwaymen accosted him with horrible oaths and demanded his money, watch and valuables. He handed over £35, his gold watch, his cloak-bag, holding linen and clothes for his wife as well as for himself, and his portmanteau, containing silver plate worth £150. They took his servant's spare clothes and the child's linen, and even threatened to kill the child unless more money was produced. Finally they rode off, leaving the post-chaise looking, said the *Western Flying Post*, like a privateer after a smart engagement at sea. Later, when Poulter confessed, he made the criminal's usual improbable excuses: Burke had initiated the hold-up; he himself had cut his hand on the coach-window in the dark and accidentally touched the cock of his pistol by a sudden movement of his hand; he had taken only six guineas and some silver; and, when the child wept in terror, he had soothed her fears by taking her from Dr Hancock and rocking her in his arms.

Tradition maintains that at this time, and for some years previously, this highwayman was living at 'the Chapel of Plaister' near Box, not far from Bath though inside Wiltshire. This building, dating back to 1450, served originally as a hospice for pilgrims to St Joseph's Chapel at Glastonbury, but after the Dissolution it became bakehouse, alehouse, barn, pigsty, in a rapidly descending scale, with its altar degraded and its walls falling into semi-ruin, before it was removed from secular use and became the restored building called Chapel Plaister today. Poulter lived, or rather came and went at frequent intervals, at the Bell, a low cottage-inn next to the ancient chapel. It was a place known to thieves, gamblers and gentlemen of the road, who were all on friendly terms with its landlord, Stephen Gee, and Mary, his wife. After the Hancock robbery, Poulter and Burke rode hard to this place, where Mary Gee stoked up the fire for them, gave them hot 'toddy' and lent Poulter a 'wallet' or bag for packing the stolen clothes, folding the gowns herself quite lovingly, because the men 'mustn't rumple them'. Gee gave them more gunpowder to make balls for reloading their pistols before they set off again. They found a man willing to buy the shirt and greatcoat of Dr Hancock's servant, knowing well that these were stolen goods, and warned the man's wife to remove the buttons and lining from the coat.

The Gees, like several of Poulter's accomplices, were arrested as a result of his confession, but he made a more horrifying revelation that finally damned him. He said that in 1749 he had murdered Dr George Shakerley, Archdeacon of Wells, at whose inquest the verdict of *felo de se* had been returned since the archdeacon had been found dead from pistol-wounds, slumped in his chair with a pistol in his hand and another on the table. Poulter had been in service for a time at Archdeacon Shakerley's and knew when he had received a large sum of money. During his master's afternoon sleep he had put the pistol into his mouth and shot him, afterwards placing the pistol in his hand.

Poulter was removed to the notorious Ilchester Gaol, on the north bank of the river Ivel, where today the green meadows show no noticeable vestige of the grim prison whose walls and floors became wringing-wet with the seepage of the river, as Henry Hunt and John Howard later reported. Here Poulter made additional disclosures of his crimes, hoping to save his life by betraying his dangerous confederates and receivers, and by naming the inns that sheltered and aided them. For a brief time he was lodged in the Bridewell at Taunton, where he wrote a flattering address to Beau Nash, who seems to have known him and to have welcomed fulsome addresses in which he figured as 'Your Honour', the writer signing himself 'Your most truly devoted and obedient servant'.

Poulter said that his friend Mary Gee had paid him half a guinea for a stolen petticoat of quilted red silk. It was for the Gees's daughter, and Mrs Gee had wheedled out of him a lace cap with a wired border to accompany the petticoat—oh yes, she had promised to alter the cap before her daughter wore it as it had come out of a portmanteau, the stolen contents of which had been widely advertised in Bath.

He had a close friend and resourceful accomplice, John Roberts, who kept the Pack Horse Inn in Bath, where Poulter generally lodged. After a robbery at Blandford, Roberts bought embroidered sheets from him (two guineas) and, for his wife, a petticoat ('worked with a needle') for one guinea (worth four); he had obligingly hidden the other stolen clothes in a closet. Roberts had often given Poulter valuable tips about customers before they left his inn; for instance, one man had just been paid £20. He personally strapped the customer's bag containing this money on his horse, so that Poulter could remove it easily when he waylaid the customer on the road. That robbery had been rather a joke, as Poulter terrified the victim by touching his cheek with a cold tinder-box, pretending it was a pistol. The Pack Horse, its landlord, his wife and many of the *clientèle* had rendered much useful service to the highwayman. Roberts and his wife were arrested; he died in Shepton Mallet gaol before his trial.

One dark night, as Poulter roamed the dimly-lit streets of Bath with a friend called Browne, he stared through a window of a house on North Parade where the curtains had not been drawn when servants lit the candles. Poulter made a sign to his companion who stared into an empty parlour and saw a trunk standing on the floor. They walked softly into the house and parlour. Poulter turned the key in the lock of the trunk and found it packed with rich clothes ready for someone's departure after a Bath season. They heard footsteps and stood silent behind the door when a servant looked in at the fire and turned back without entering. Somehow they carried out the trunk unnoticed while the family were at dinner and took it to Kingsmead Fields.

154

Poulter put the fine clothes into a sack and despatched Browne on horseback with them to a suitable destination.

As for horses, he had stolen dozens: from Somerset farmers on market-day, from Somerset fairs and after races that he attended in two or three western counties. (He was born at Newmarket.) Once, at the Green Dragon in Crewkerne, he learned that two accomplices had become alarmed and fled, leaving their two stolen horses behind. Poulter and his fellow coolly collected them, a gelding and a mare, and rode them to Bath, fearing all the way that they would be stopped. They sold the gelding to a know-ledgeable man for 36s; he said they were 'stolen far enough off' for him to hazard selling the horse to an unsuspecting farmer outside Bath who supplied him with straw.

No criminal was more endangered by Poulter's sworn state-ment before a Devon Justice of the Peace than his extremely useful accomplice, John Ford, the Bath silversmith, who with his wife, Betty, had helped Poulter dispose of his most precious loot —articles of gold and silver taken from rich travellers. After a robbery, the highwayman rode to Bath as swiftly as circumstances allowed and passed to the silversmith the watches, gold chains, gold and silver buckles, and gold seals that panic-stricken coach-passengers had handed over. John Ford knew where to sell these, but more identifiable pieces, such as silver tankards and plate stolen from great houses, could not be disposed of. Ford melted these down in his crucibles, aided by his wife, who told Poulter, 'Any time I will melt something', asking only a shilling for herself. The betrayed couple were arrested, but surprisingly Ford was granted bail.

In August 1753 John Poulter was tried for the robbery of Dr Hancock, at Wells Assizes, before Mr Baron Smythe and Mr Baron Adams, who sentenced him to death and to hanging in chains at the scene of the robbery. They then returned him to Ilchester Gaol, where throughout his stay he had 'behaved very bold and impudent' according to reports. He believed that his evidence against his confederates had earned him His Majesty's gracious pardon, and the *Bath Journal* concurred with this, stating that Poulter had been 'of very great service to the public' by making 'discoveries of divers robberies, receivers of stolen goods, and the inns which harbour highwaymen'. A number of Taunton inhabitants petitioned for his release. Poulter certainly performed one beneficent deed during his imprisonment after trial. The Ilchester prisoners lay on straw in their wretched wards, being allowed ten pounds of clean straw every week; if they were lucky, they had a candle for light after the turnkey locked their wards at sunset. A woman in a back ward fell asleep with her candle burning and knocked it over on the straw. Poulter rescued her from the flames and, although she suffered burns and both of them nearly suffocated, he prevented a bigger catastrophe. Luckily this prison fire did not break out on one of the many nights when the turnkey locked up the wards and went off outside Ilchester for several hours with the key of the main door in his pocket—which, as protesting prisoners swore to magistrates, was his practice.

In February 1754, on a Sunday, Poulter staged a most daring escape from the prison, a feat that people found almost impossible to credit. Although he had received respites, he was under sentence of death and, because of his known audacity and dangerous character, was lodged in the most secure quarters, under constant watch. He had 'irons' on both legs, which his jailers testified to be badly 'galled from the irons'; moreover, he was chained to a debtor-prisoner called Newman—who escaped with him. They pulled out an iron bar, got through the window on to the roof, tied a rope lengthened by Poulter's garters to a chimney, slid down it and, when it broke, fell down on the wall of a Mr Tucker's garden and got clear away. Somehow Poulter dragged himself ten miles before obtaining an implement to free himself of the leg irons. Afterwards he reached Wookey, near Wells, where on the Wednesday he was captured. When carried before the Dean of Wells he declared—quite falsely, so Cox and Clothier, his agitated jailers, swore—that his jailers had accepted twenty guineas to let him escape. He was taken back to Ilchester. His execution was now smartly expedited and on the Sunday evening Clothier went to read his death warrant to him. According to him, Poulter wept and said, 'God's will be done', before begging forgiveness for his false statement about connivance.

Parson Bowyer, of Martock, who administered the sacrament to the highwayman on the morning of execution, said that he found him resigned and even cheerful. Certainly he seemed devoid of all fear of death and staged a dramatic, even heroic end in front of the great crowd which gathered at Ilchester to witness the hanging of such a celebrity. They murmured admiration as he rode along in the cart, and stood tall and upright to address them. In the throng he spied Ford, the Bath silversmith, who having escaped his own punishment, had come to watch him die. In ringing tones Poulter again denounced this accomplice, swearing that in his written confession he had not declared a hundredth of 'that gang's villainies'. He laid his hands on the coffin and cried, 'Welcome Death, by the grace of God', then leaped on to the coffin and helped the executioner 'rope him up as short as he could'. Finally, before the cart could be pulled from under him, he threw himself off with a last disdainful gesture.

An even greater crowd, composed of citizens of Bath, inhabitants of Claverton, Galhampton and neighbouring villages, and burgesses of Bradford-on-Avon, assembled on Claverton Down to see the body of John Poulter, alias Baxter, drawn up, encased in an iron cage, to hang in chains from a gibbet near the place where he had robbed Dr Hancock on a dark, windy March night. The gibbet stood at the side of the turnpike-road not far from the entry to Lime Kiln Lane that runs out from Claverton village on to the top of the down. There his body hung until his skeleton disintegrated, a reminder of formidable retribution to other highwaymen.

JACK WHITE

Jack White created his humble and ignoble legend nearly 250

years ago. Unlike the story of another rustic murderer, John Walford, the charcoal-burner of Over Stowey in the Quantocks, which originated some fifty years later, it did not remain plain and unadorned by fanciful trimmings. Even the region to which Jack White's tale belongs came to give more credence to the contrived and elaborated version that makes coincidence stretch a very long arm. However, it never had the poignancy of the charcoal-burner's story, which relates how John Walford was executed, on the lower slope of Danesborough in the Quantock Hills, for the murder of his half-witted wife. The parish had forced him to marry her, although he loved the miller's daughter, who at the end knelt with him on the straw in the executioner's cart. Each of these men left his gibbet as a grim memorial that stood near the wayside for many years. Walford's Gibbet is now a grassy place, marked on the ordnance map, in the parish of Over Stowey off the A39 road, about fifteen miles from Mine-head. Jack White's Gibbet is a crossroads, also marked on the map, where the lower road from Castle Cary to Wincanton cuts across the old Portway in the parish of Bratton Seymour.

Jack White was born at Wincanton in 1690 and baptised in the parish church of St Peter and St Paul. The population numbered only 1,500, but work was not scarce as Wincanton had a thriving little weaving industry. Jack White, however, although born to hardworking parents, grew up an idler. He was never in regular employment but drifted from one odd job to another, even after his marriage to a gentle industrious girl, Sarah Slade, who bore him a child that died. He squandered much of his money and time on sports like cock-fighting, that took place in the courtyards of local inns; became a hard drinker, and continually hung about inns and alehouses, where he sometimes earned a shilling or two by carrying coach passengers' luggage or helping the ostler. The Sun Inn became his favourite rendezvous for drink, companionship and hearing news of the outside world from overnight travellers.

It was the summer of 1730, a summer of scorching heat when

drought bleached the meadows, withered wild flowers and hedge-rows, and dried up ponds and pools. Work became a burden and tempers frayed easily; it was an even greater pleasure than usual to loll on a settle, drinking ale or cider in the cool, flagstone-floored premises of the Sun. On a late afternoon of sultry heat, the landlord, Mr Gilbert, stood at his door, encouraging several of his acquaintances to come in for a drink and be entertained by various items of news recounted by Robert Sutton, a young man who had paused for a meal and a few hours' rest before the final stage of his journey to a gentleman's house near Castle Cary, where he had to deliver an important letter. Jack White, who needed no persuasion to enter the inn, slaked his thirst with cider as he listened to Sutton giving a respectful group of customers a commentary on past and forthcoming events in other Somerset towns. A judge named Lee, he said, had been appointed to go on the Western Circuit, and Mr Baron Thompson would assist him. Whereupon a Wincanton youth, trying to be witty, remarked that nobody would be surprised if Jack White came up at the Assizes to answer for his sins to Mr Baron Thompson. This raised a general laugh, but Jack White flushed darkly at the joke and started to pick a quarrel. Bob Sutton quietened him by buying him another drink, producing a well-filled pouch when he paid. White subsided sullenly on to the settle and continued drinking until Sutton jumped up and remarked that soon it would be dusk, he had a letter to deliver and did not know the way. Would Jack White walk with him and show him the house? After another mug of cider White consented, but it was obvious, when he left the inn with Sutton, that hard drinking had in-creased the blackness of his mood.

A sultry dark-grey sky pressed down on the earth and the heavy heat weighed on both men. After walking a mile or two, they lay down on the verge of the highway and went to sleep, hoping to clear their heads and wake to a cool breeze. It was the sound of women's voices and laughter that roused them as two young women approached from the Castle Cary direction. Jack

159

White got up and slouched across to meet them. He accosted them boldly and one of them was responsive enough to let him kiss her. He then attempted to kiss her companion, who struggled and screamed for help so that Sutton came up, pulled White roughly away and ordered him to come on. As the women hurried off White grew truculent, shouting abuse and putting up his fists. Bob Sutton dealt with him harshly, insisting with curses that White must continue the journey. Finally he showed White a gilded token from Nuremberg in his cupped hand, swearing that it was a half-guinea which they would spend together after delivering his letter. So they trudged on until they came to the crossroads for Castle Cary, Holton, Bratton Seymour and Wincanton. Here Bob Sutton declared himself dead-beat and, stretching himself on the grass, fell into another heavy sleep. White lay down near him and stared at the sleeper with sullen envy as he remembered the shining 'half-guinea' and the pouch apparently stuffed with more. He got up, tore a stake from the hedge and beat Bob Sutton savagely about the head. Sutton struggled to rise and fight, then fell back silenced by another heavy blow.

Jack White dragged the body under a furze-bush and took possession of the pouch. Then panic seized him. Darkness was falling; he must hurry away, but first he must conceal his victim's body. Frantically he tried to dig a hollow in the ground with his bare hands, but drought had made it as hard as iron. He climbed a stile into a field and peered into a pond, but it had dried up and there was insufficient water to cover a body. He pulled the corpse into a dry ditch and hurried home in the darkening night.

On 6 August 1730, he faced Mr Baron Thompson at Bridgwater Assizes and was sentenced to be hanged on the site of his crime. He made no defence except that 'the hounds of hell were after me'. His execution took place on a Wincanton market-day a fortnight later, in front of an assembled crowd of market-folk, weavers, farmers and tradesmen from Wincanton and Castle Cary. They surged round the hangman's cart uttering loud execrations, for they knew that in Ilchester Gaol White had made a full written confession. This was printed in the *Whitehall Evening Post* for 29 August. In it White stated that 'one Gilbert at the Sign of the Sun' had called him into his house and that Robert Sutton 'with cursing and oaths had sworn a counter was a half-guinea even he would spend on me'.

The elaborated version of this simple, sordid tale would have it believed that Jack White's family were decayed gentry, descended from a family called Leblanc. The supposed ancestral home where he and his younger brother William were born still exists in Wincanton, having survived the eighteenth-century fire that destroyed many of the town's old buildings, some of which were replaced by handsome inns and houses designed by the architect, Nathaniel Ireson, who lived in Wincanton. It is a very pleasing Jacobean manor-house of yellow-brown stone, with mullions of golden Ham stone to its latticed windows, a gabled roof of russet-brown tiles and a three-storeyed porch overlooking the forecourt. One room facing the street is called the Orange Room because William of Orange received hospitality here soon after landing in England. The house still keeps the quaint name of 'The Dogs', by which it was known in the days of William, though it has now lost the two stone dogs on the stone gateposts, from which the name originated. Its entrance faces the road down Tout Hill, which is a continuation of South Street, the house being on the summit of the steep ascent from the lower town. It was said that the White parents fell into poverty, the father died, then the mother and her sons had to leave the mansion for a cottage and lead the life of the struggling poor. Jack was an encumbrance because of his idleness and dissipation, but brave adventurous William went to sea at sixteen on board the privateer *Rover*, and during twenty years was never heard of. When his mother died, Jack White and his wife Sarah had only the few shillings he earned carrying luggage for passengers on the London stage-coach. The pretty old coaching-inn called the Bear, now the Bear Hotel, was built in his lifetime. His old school-friend, Richard Palmer, became landlord of the George

Inn at Castle Cary and, in spite of White's laziness and drinking habits, gave him, for old times' sake, the regular if lowly job of ostler which meant that he had to sleep in the loft over the stables. This inn was also patronised by gentry of the neighbourhood, for Parson Woodforde records dining there with Sir Charles Tynte and other Somerset gentlemen. It has survived to become the pleasant comfortable George Hotel of today, a charming old building, long, low, with thatched roof and a sign, ornamented with fine ironwork, displaying St George on his steed killing the vanquished green dragon. Inside, the rooms and passages have uneven floors, unexpected steps and corners.

On a wild wet October evening a traveller entered the George, flung himself down on a bench and ordered cold beef, bread and beer. The room where he took his refreshment looks out on the pillared Market House across the street; built in 1855 it retains the Tuscan pillars of an earlier Market House familiar to Jack White. The Castle Cary customers stared curiously at the stranger who informed them that he had travelled far and was dog-tired, but must cover the ten miles to Wincanton that night. He wore a sailor's clothes and gold earrings, had a seamed face swarthy with sunburn, and carried a small portmanteau. He asked several questions about Castle Cary and Wincanton, seemed rather curious about big houses like 'The Dogs' and their owners, and drank very freely. He paid for a round of drinks in which he included the shaggy-headed ostler, who lounged in the doorway, listening to the seaman's stories about fights with the Spaniards and the looting of Spanish towns. The ostler, like all the others, stared enviously when the stranger produced a plump leather pouch and shook out a gold Spanish coin, telling the landlord he was sorry that he had no money except Spanish doubloons, of which he had brought home a bagful, as well as valuable ornaments seized in raids on Spanish dwellings and churches. More traveller's tales and more drinking followed, and darkness was gathering when the boastful sailor left the George and, with a reeling gait, took the road to Wincanton. The sound of rain driven by a wild wind drowned all other noises.

Next morning an unknown man in sailor's garb was found dead under a furze-bush at the crossroads. Landlord Richard Palmer recognised his customer of the previous night, and said that a portmanteau and a pouch of Spanish money had been taken. Stab wounds in the sailor's body proved that the thief had murdered him. The crime horrified the entire neighbourhood and all the inhabitants co-operated with magistrates and clergy in trying to find the murderer. Not a man refused to take part in the 'trial by ordeal'.

The sailor's shrouded corpse lay in an open coffin inside the main entrance to Wincanton parish church. This was the door of the Perpendicular west tower standing then at the west end of the nave, but now at the west end of the north aisle and the only surviving portion of the old church, which underwent eighteenth-century alteration and Victorian rebuilding. It is not possible now to enter through this iron-studded door, as the entrance has been considerably raised. Here, in a gloom almost unrelieved by daylight, the white-haired vicar in his vestments stood with a magistrate behind the coffin, while man after man obeyed the vicar's solemn summons to come forward from the awestruck crowd outside to touch the corpse: the victim's wounds would bleed if the murderer laid his hands on the body. Halfway through the macabre proceeding, people turned their heads because of a disturbance. Richard Palmer, of the George at Castle Cary, was pulling an ashen-faced, reluctant Jack White up the path, and then pushing him forward, telling him to do his duty like the rest instead of cowering in the background. 'You must touch him, Jack.'

'If innocent, you have nothing to fear,' the old vicar said.

They noticed that sweat stood on White's forehead as he reached out a shaking hand and touched the dead sailor's breast. They shuddered, gasped, then let out an ominous cry as a trickle of blood flowed from the dead man's mouth.

Jack White was seized and handed over to the constables. They found his clasp-knife on him and a stain on his sleeve. His bed of hay in the loft over the stables was searched, and revealed a handful of hay that had wiped his bloody knife, a bag of gold Spanish doubloons and the sailor's portmanteau. As a crowning dramatic event, the portmanteau was found to contain, among other personal belongings, a Bible with a sheet of paper pasted inside its cover, bearing these words:

Wincanton February 2nd 1692
William, the son of John and Mary White, was baptised here this day by me
(Signed) George Plucknett, Curate
(Signed) Thos. Green, Clerk

Jack White had killed his long-lost brother, who had returned home with his savings hoping to help his family! The murderer dropped like a stone when he learned the truth. Every man expressed the utmost hatred and aversion for him. Justice added a final ignominy to the death sentence, decreeing that, after execution at the first crossroads between Castle Cary and Wincanton, the body should hang 'in chains' as a horrible warning to all who passed by.

The Wincanton blacksmith made the iron cage to fit the body, which was drawn up high on the gibbet-arm and left to swing on creaking chains throughout the year, while kites and carrion crows picked the bones, and rain and wind bleached them, till they fell, bit by bit, on the ground below. The gibbet-post stood until 1840. During the long years, passers-by on dark nights heard the creak of chains and sometimes a voice moaning 'Jack's cold, terrible cold!'—as one of Parson Woodforde's hard-drinking relatives from Castle Cary testified. Down the years people told their children the story of Jack White, the ostler, who—tempted by the gleam of Spanish gold—hurried from the inn and hid in the dark behind a furze-thicket at the mouth of the narrow lane to Bratton Seymour, until he heard the singing sailor approaching. He meant to stun him with his cudgel, but stabbed him when he put up a fight.

After a time an enclosed coppice was planted on the piece of green wasteland where the gibbet stood stark and prominent. The modern signpost, which is more or less on the gibbet's site, stands on a grass verge back from an extremely busy road, although green fields and groups of trees lie all around. Behind the signpost a thick, tall hedge stretches to the opening of the Bratton Seymour lane, above a ditch full of purple deadnettle, thistles and hogweed. There is a single oak tree.

The stump of the gibbet was uprooted one night in 1840 by young revellers who carried it to an inn at Galhampton and burnt it on the fire, with little thought of Jack White or his sailor victim, as they drank their ale. Whichever version of the legend is accepted—and it cannot be disputed that Jack White was hanged here on 19 August 1730—his last confession carried a touching tribute to his wife:

'I beg the world not to cast reflections on my dear and innocent wife who has behaved herself with great tenderness to me, even in a common Gaol.'

165

Bibliography

BOOKS

Anon	*A Compleat History of Somersetshire* (Sherborne, 1742)
Alcock, L.	*Arthur's Britain* (1971)
Ashe, G. (ed)	*The Quest for Arthur's Britain* (1968)
Atthill, R.	*Old Mendip* (Newton Abbot, 1964)
Balch, H.	*Caves of Mendip* (1929)
Baring-Gould, S. and Fisher, J.	*Lives of the British Saints* (1907-13)
Barker, R. W.	*Arthur of Albion* (1961)
Bazell, C.	*The Edington Campaign* (1955)
Boger, Mrs E.	*Myths, Scenes & Worthies of Somerset* (1887)
Boumphrey, G.	*Along the Roman Roads* (1935)
Chambers, E. K.	*Arthur of Britain* (1927)

166

Chenevix-Trench, C. *The Western Rising* (1969)
Collingwood, R. G. *Roman Britain* (Oxford, 1936)
  and Myres, J. N. L
Collinson, J. *History of Somersetshire* (1791)
Couzens, P. *Bruton in Selwood* (Sherborne, 1968)
Curtis, C. D. *Sedgemoor and the Bloody Assize* (1930)
Cuzner, S. Handbook to Frome-Selwood (Frome,
  1865)

Davis, F. Rose, G., *The Shepton Mallet Story* (Shepton
  and Hopper, M. Mallet, 1969)
Dobson, D. *The Archaeology of Somerset* (1931)

Earle, J. *The Alfred Jewel* (Oxford, 1901)
Earle, J. *Bath Guide* (1767)

Farbrother, J. *Shepton Mallet* (1859)
Fea, A. *King Monmouth* (1902)

Greenwood, C. and J.*Somerset Delineated* (1822)
Greswell, W. *Dumnonia and the Valley of the Parret*
  (Taunton, 1922)
Greswell, W. *The Battle of Edington* (Taunton, 1910)

Hearne, T. (ed) *History and Antiquities of Glastonbury—*
  John of Glastonbury (1722)
Helm, P. *Alfred the Great* (1963)
Hole, C. *Saints in Folklore* (1966)
Hole, C. *English Folk-Heroes* (1948)
Hutchings, M. *Inside Somerset* (Sherborne, 1963)
Hutton, E. *Highways and Byways in Somerset* (1912)

Jarman *History of Bridgwater* (1889)

Knight, F. A. *Heart of Mendip* (1915)

167

Lewis, L.	*St Joseph of Arimathea at Glastonbury* (1922)
Lewis, L.	*Glastonbury, The Mother of Saints* (1925)
Little, B.	*The Monmouth Episode* (1951)
Locke, R.	*The Western Rebellion* (Taunton, 1885)
MacMillan, D.	*Jack White's Gibbet* (Somerset Folk Press, 1922)
Malmesbury, William of	*Antiquities of Glastonbury* (trans F. Lomax, 1908)
Malmesbury, William of	*History of the Kings of England* (c 1140) (trans J. A. Giles, 1847)
Marson, C. L.	*Glastonbury or the English Jerusalem* (1925)
Melville, L.	*Mr Crofts the King's Bastard* (1929)
Monmouth, Geoffrey of	*History of the Kings of Britain* (trans Lewis Thorpe, 1966)
Page, M.	*The Battle of Sedgemoor* (Bridgwater, 1930)
Peach, R. E.	*Bath Old and New* (1888)
Peach, R. E.	*Annals of Swainswick* (1890)
Pevsner, N.	*North Somerset* (1958)
Pevsner, N.	*South West Somerset* (1958)
Phelps, W.	*History and Antiquities of Somersetshire* (1839)
Piggott, S.	*British Prehistory* (1949)
Poole, C. H.	*Customs, Superstitions and Legends of the County of Somerset* (1877)
Pooley, C.	*Old Stone Crosses of Somerset* (1877)
Porter, H. M.	*The Saxon Conquest of Somerset & Devon* (Bath, 1967)
Pring, D. J.	*The Saxon Conquest of Somerset* (Taunton, 1933)

Radford, J. Ralegh	*Glastonbury Abbey* (1970)
Roberts, G.	*Life of James, Duke of Monmouth* (1844)
Robinson, J. Armitage	*Somerset Historical Essays* (1921)
Robinson, J. Armitage	*The Times of St Dunstan* (1923)
Robinson, J. Armitage	*Two Glastonbury Legends* (Oxford, 1926)
Smith, R. L.	*Bath* (1944)
Snell, F. J.	*King Arthur's Country* (1926)
Stevens-Cox, J.	*Ilchester Gaol and House of Correction* (Ilchester, 1949)
Stradling, W.	*A Description of the Priory of Chilton-super-Polden* (Bridgwater, 1839)
Sweetman, G.	*History of Wincanton* (1903)
Tate, W. J.	*Somerset in Bygone Days* (1912)
Toulmin, J.	*History of Taunton* (1822)
Treharne, R. F.	*The Glastonbury Legends* (1966)
Walters, C.	*Bygone Somerset* (1897)
Warner, C. J.	*History of Bath* (1801)
Watson, J. Willis (ed)	*Calendar of Somerset Customs & Superstitions* (reprinted from the *Somerset County Herald*, 1920)
Wood, J.	*A Description of Bath* (1765)
Wood, F. H.	*Somerset Memories & Traditions* (1924)
Wright, R. W. M.	*Bath Abbey* (1968)

PERIODICALS AND JOURNALS

PSAS=*Proceedings of the Somerset Archaeological Society.*

Alcock, L.	'Excavations at South Cadbury Castle', *PSAS* 114 (1970)

Alford, R.   'The Milkmaid and the Battlefield',
                          Somerset Year Book (1925)

Baines, W.   'Ealahelm', *PSAS* 20 (1874)
Bates, J. Harbin   'Leland in Somersetshire', *PSAS* 33
                          (1887)
Batten, E. C.   'The Holy Thorn', *PSAS* 26 (1880)
Bennett, J. A.   'Camelot', *PSAS* 36 (1890)
Broadbent, M.   'Apostle unto Britain', *The Cornish
                          Review* (Spring 1969)

Freeman, E. A.   'King Ine', Part I *PSAS* 26 (1880)

Gray, St G.   'Cadbury Castle', *PSAS* 59 (1913)
Gray, St G.   'Battlegore, Williton', PSAS 78 (1932)
Green, J.   'Dunstan', *PSAS* 11 (1861)
Grenville, R. N.   'Somerset Drainage', PSAS 72 (1926)
Grinsell, L. V.   'Somerset Barrows', *PSAS* 113 (1969)

Hardman, J. W.   'The Hagiology of Somerset', *PSAS* 12
                          (1887)
Horne, Dom E.   'Somerset Holy Wells', *Somerset Folk
                          Series* No 12 (1923)

Jones, W. A.   'On the Reputed Discovery of King
                          Arthur's Remains at Glastonbury',
                          PSAS 9 (1859)

Mathews, F. W.   'Tales of the Blackdown Borderland',
                          Somerset Folk Series No 13 (1923)
Morland, J.   'Pomparles, Glastonbury', *PSAS* 58 (1912)
Morland, J.   'On an ancient Road between Glastonbury
                          and Street', *PSAS* 27 (1881)
Morland, J.   'The Brue at Glastonbury', *PSAS* 68
                          (1922)

Palmer, H. P.   'Old Somerset', *Somerset Folk Series*
                       No 20 (1925)

Radford, C. Ralegh   'The Church in Somerset down to 1100',
                       PSAS 106 (1961-2)
Rahtz, P.   'Cannington Hillfort', *PSAS* 113 (1969)
Rahtz, P.   'Excavations at Chalice Well', *PSAS* 108
                       (1964)
Rahtz, P.   'The Saxon & Medieval Palaces at Ched-
                       dar', *PSAS* 108 (1964)
Robinson, J.   'Memories of St Dunstan in Somerset',
   Armitage   PSAS 62 (1916)

Stubbs, (ed)   'Memorials of St Dunstan', *Rolls Series*

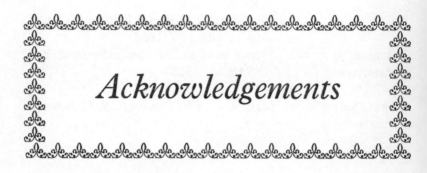

Acknowledgements

The author would like to make grateful acknowledgement to the librarians and staffs of the Somerset County Library and Bridgwater Borough Library for help so readily given on many occasions, and also to the librarian and staff of Bath City Reference Library for assistance. Thanks are due also to the curator of the Blake Museum, Bridgwater, for permission to photograph certain objects in the museum, and to the Worshipful Company of Goldsmiths for permission to reproduce the photograph of the figure of St Dunstan. The author gratefully acknowledges the permission granted by Charles Causley for the use of the extract from his 'Ballad of Samuel Sweet', *Figure of Eight* (Macmillan, 1969).

ADDENDA

A shrine in the cathedral at St Davids, Pembrokeshire, contains St David's bones.

According to a recent book *Drawings of Baltonsborough* by M. Somers Cocks and G. Paton, St Dunstan was born in the hamlet of Ham Street at Baltonsborough.

The stout dead trunk of Monmouth's Tree now lies on a field-slope behind the manor-house at Whitelackington.

Index

Note: Saints' names are listed alphabetically preceded by St; page numbers in italics indicate plates

Parcet, Elizabeth, 109
Parrett, River, 12, 14, 20, 25, 77, 78, 79, 82, 87
Patwell, 35
Pawlett, 12
Penselwood, 32
Pilgrims' Way, 13, 14
Pilton, 18, 19, 20
Pitminster, 122
Pixies' Mound, 81-2
Pixy Piece, 81
Plumley, George, 123, 124
Polden Hills, 12, 21, 77, 82, 86, 88, 110, 111
Pomparles (Pons Perilis), 13, 73, 74, 74
Porlock, 64
Portman, Sir William, 108
Poulter, John (Baxter), 150-7; travels, 151; robberies, 151; robs Dr Hancock, 151-2; his confederates, the Gees, 153; murder of Dr Shakerley, robberies at Bath, 154; trial at Wells, 155; escape from Ilchester Gaol, 156; execution, 157
Priddy, 22, 24, 27
Purbeck, Isle of, 40
Puriton, 13, 14

Quantock Hills, 21, 71, 77, 79, 86, 100, 101, 158

Red-Leg Johnnies, 141-2
Righton's Grave, 88
Rowe, Elizabeth, 125-6

Sealey, Mr, 140, 141
Sedgemoor, 19, 21, 87, 105, 106, 111, 118, 120, 121, 122

Sedgemoor Runner, 12
Selwood, Forest of, 32, 33, 34, 35, 36, 37, 86
Shakerley, Dr, 153
Shapwick, 120
Shepton Mallet, 38, 117, 154
Shervage Wood, 100
St Sidwell, 81, 82
Solsbury Hill, 59
South Cadbury, 70
Speke, Charles, 130, 131
Speke, George, 129
Speke, John, 118, 130
Stawell, Lord, (1) 131
Stawell, Lord, (2) 102, 103
Stert, 80
Stockland, 80
Stocklinch, 137-40
Stoke Lane (Stoke St Michael), 53, 54
Stolford, 81
Stonedown, 15
Street, 9, 10, 13, 67, 73
Strode, Edward, 117
Strode, William, 139
Sutton Montis, 71, 72
Swainswick, 60, 61, 69
Swayne, Jan, 122
Sydenham Manor, 119, 120

Tarry House, 111
Taunton, 86, 104, 105, 111, 114, 118, 124, 125, 127, 129, 133, 134, 135, 136, 140
Taunton Castle, 129, 140
Thorne, 148
Three Greyhounds Inn, 127
Timsbury, 113
Tone, River, 77, 78
Tootle Bridge, 44
Turn Hill, 21
Tynte, Sir Charles, 147, 162